FAITH THROUGH
REASON

Previously published in the follow editions:
Tyngdepunktet: Hvorfor jeg ble katolikk Genesis Forlag, Oslo, 2002
Akit az igazság megtalált Helikon, Budapest, 2002
El amor escondido Belacqua, Barcelona, 2002
Inna Love Story W drodze, Poznan, 2002
Love-Story: So wurde ich katholisch Sankt Ulrich Verlag, 2003
Quand raison et foi se recontrent Presses de la Renaissance,
Paris, 2003
Una scelta d'amore Leonardo International, Milano, 2004
Nenavadna ljubezenska zgodba Mohorjeva, Ljubljana, 2005

Thanks are due to Kate and Louis Marcelin Rice for their help in
the translation of the Preface by Cardinal Joseph Ratzinger,
taken from the Italian edition of this book *Una scelta d'amore*.

FAITH THROUGH REASON

Janne Haaland Matláry

GRACEWING

This edition published in 2006
by
Gracewing
2 Southern Avenue,
Leominster
Herefordshire HR6 0QF

ISBN 0 85244 004 9
ISBN 978 0 85244 004 9

Typeset by Action Publishing Technology Ltd,
Gloucester GL1 5SR

To my parents

CONTENTS

PREFACE

What led a young Norwegian woman, who grew up with
a deep love for the rugged and majestic scenery of her
native land, and was educated in its secular, post-
Protestant culture, to become a Catholic? This book
recounts the various stages of that adventurous journey.
Janne Haaland Matláry's love for the unspoiled scenery of
her homeland was matched by her passion for research
and her joy in exploring areas of knowledge which take us
by surprise, forcing us to ask ourselves ever bigger questions. For Janne the many and various questions which
presented themselves in the course of her journey
converge in a single fundamental question: is it possible to
know the Truth? Or is everything relative? Thus her quest
led her to philosophy and, since she was determined not
to become imprisoned in an ivory tower of mere specula-
tion, from philosophy to political theory. The question of
Truth – can it be known, or is it absolutely impenetrable?
– acquires here a concrete dimension. In a constitutional
state can one put a limit on the principle of majoritarian-
ism? Or is such a limit now inconceivable – the view of the
Uppsala School? Is there no connection between ethics
and law? Is law really nothing more than an expression of
the will of the majority?
  The idea implies a contempt for the dignity of the
human condition and nullifies both law and the human
state. Janne addressed this problem in her distinguished
master's thesis, treating a topic that is both profoundly

practical and philosophical at the same time. Since philosophy was not taught in Norway's higher education institutes, she enrolled at Augsburg, a Lutheran college in the western United States, where she became acquainted with the great philosophers of the past whose thinking has helped to shape law and politics – Aristotle, Plato, Plotinus and Thomas Aquinas. Paradoxically, it was at Augsburg she got to know a Catholic professor who not only helped her to become familiar with the great philosophers but also taught her a Catholicism that was above all an intellectual, philosophical system. Of this period of her development, she writes: 'In all these academic discussions, my greatest problem ... was that of subjectivity. Far from being applicable only to academia, however, this question was the key to giving meaning to life'. In every era men have derived a powerful intellectual stimulus from the great synthesis of fundamental questions on human existence, from Plato and Aristotle to Thomas Aquinas, and the author of this book is no exception. Yes, truth exists and it is possible to know it, even if only in a fragmentary way: this was the conviction that grew within her. Thus, she became a 'Thomist', or at least she considers herself as such. Though strongly attracted to Christianity as a philosophical system, she nevertheless experienced an irreconcilable gulf between herself and the day-to-day life of the Church. 'I thought at length about what to do. Why not simply leave things as they were? I was not Christian and would never have been. I liked the liturgy and the music, the culture of Catholicism and its ethical system. But becoming Catholic was something else.'

Another door opened when, in Oslo, Janne met a French Dominican with whom she had regular weekly discussions over a period of eighteen months. At first they were purely philosophical in character, but as time passed they became discourses on the faith in the course of which something unexpected became clear to her: the Truth is a person and that person is Christ. And this conviction gradually took firmer and firmer hold. Janne herself wrote, 'Today I understood that in the consecrated host there is an objective reality, which is independent of my own opinion or whether or not I believe in it.' For her this realisation was something akin to a Copernican revolution. From then on, more and more often in church before the red light symbolising the Lord's presence, the reality of it overwhelmed her. 'Understanding this truth was a grace that could only flourish where the ground was fertile.'

Eventually the moment came, at Easter 1982, when Janne took the step of converting to the Catholic Church. She was then twenty-five. The knowledge that she had discovered the truth, or rather that it had discovered her – the sense of being taken by surprise – was itself overwhelming. Becoming one with revealed truth was like being touched by and filled with a long-sought-after love. Truth was revealed in the form of love. 'Those who have only just entered the Church usually show all the symptoms of being in love', writes the author, and she returns several times to this analogy, comparing the experience of truth revealed with the happiness that comes from being loved. In other words: faith is joy, and joy is the fruit of love. She quotes Chesterton who, on being asked what had impelled him to become a Catholic, replied 'because I wanted to be happy'.

This is something very different from mere infatuation. Conversion (*conversio*), Janne tells us – echoing the experience of all the great converts – is not the exaltation of a moment, nor even a point of arrival, 'but a process that lasts a lifetime. Nothing is ever certain along this path ... It is necessary to renew one's own will to convert every day, and this means starting and restarting from the beginning'. She reminds us of some truths that we all know but too often ignore: the importance of a constant inner life, the need to 'train' ourselves in Christ. The image of falling in love thus acquires greater profundity: 'I think it is possible to draw a parallel between being in love and being married ... A married person who has managed to stay married is probably no longer in love, but loves in a more mature and altruistic way.'

The Christian adventure lies in this impetus of love, in

experiencing its continuous joy and bringing it to full maturity. Janne Matláry tells us how, very slowly, she reached this second conversion, moving on from being just a 'Sunday Christian' to experience the mutual inter-penetration of faith and daily life. This second adventure, though less spectacular, less dazzling, is the greater and more profound.

The whole structure of the faith and of Catholic life are present in the various stages of Janne's journey towards conversion, and through her book, we can, so to speak, learn afresh what it means to be a Catholic. Many Catholics lead lives that bear no relation to the experience of falling in love. Theirs are the routine habits of tired conjugal relationships from which all traces of initial enthusiasm have vanished and even love seems to have frozen. A joyless life. Thanks to this book, it is possible to return to the state of 'first love', to experience once again the greatness and daring of the 'yes' of Catholics, its vast-ness, its light, and the joy that strengthens us on the precarious path of faith, and keeps intact the intensity of that first love which alone can show us the way to the summit.

That is why I hope this book will have the widest possi-ble distribution.

Cardinal Joseph Ratzinger

CHAPTER 1

HAPPY TIMES

We seem to live in happy times in the West. We have material prosperity, unparalleled in history. We live longer, are taller, and control our lives more than at any time before. We seem to be the true masters of our own destiny. We are better educated than any generation before us, and technology and medicine have progressed to an astonishing degree.

From the post-war generation until today there seems to have been a steady line of progress. We have undone the tyrants. We have democracy in all western states. We can decide ourselves on our social, economic, and political fate.

We ought to live in happy times.

The freedom we enjoy is also unparalleled: traditional expectations of how we should live have disappeared. In fact, nothing handed down by tradition has any authority over us. This is seen as great progress by most people.

What characterises our time? How is it different from earlier times? Is it better now than before? In short, are we happier now? There is of course no definite answer to the last question, but I think that we can safely say that there is a discrepancy between our material progress, which is undisputable, and our degree of human happiness, which is somehow unrelated to things.

The natural instinct of man is to seek happiness. Ultimately, deep down, we want more than material satisfaction, and today there is a tremendous search for meaning – in new ways, by new means. This is sympto-matic of the need to find happiness.

But at the same time there is a thorough materialism about life. Old ties of community and family erode, and the single person lives basically for himself. One can have an entirely *autistic* life in society, living for onself only, in one's own universe. The centre of life, its very meaning, seems to be me, my own person. I must be successful, happy, satisfied; protect myself against sickness, old age and most of all, death. And there are no obvious tasks – society and family do not need me. This is especially pronounced for young people.

Our time – my time, the time of the post-war period, of the generation of the 60s and 70s – is marked by three features: *materialism, subjectivism, and utilitarianism.*

Materialism is both about having and buying, about consuming. But it is also about seeing persons as mere objects, as things. *Subjectivism* is about seeing everything in relation to the own self; deciding that nothing exists outside the self, and that no norms of right and wrong exist in themselves. My opinion about these matters is all there can be. *Utilitarianism* is about using others to our own advantage; we calculate about people: are they useful to us?

These features are much more evident today than in my parent's generation, during the war. We seek meaning in ourselves, in our self-fulfilment. Everything revolves around the self.

But happiness is not there.

Nothing but Material Reality

Materialism is no newcomer to the West. It has always been a steady incentive for human activity, and as such, is useful. But today the pressure of consuming and buying seems to be much stronger than ever before. The market logic of buying and selling is everywhere, penetrating virtually all spheres of society. My children are bombarded by advertisements, and constantly crave new things and new clothes. It is also much easier to acquire these things, which has the effect that they lose their value to us. We simply don't appreciate things that are too easily acquired.

Material progress has been a prime goal in our lives in the entire post-war period. When I was little, I remember how my mother – and the other housewives in the neighbourhood – discussed what new furniture they could buy this year; which new car; which new clothes, and so on. Status was measured in these show-pieces of progress. Norwegian society was very egalitarian, but this also meant that all families could acquire the same things. This was tangible progress in the post-war era, modelled on the dream of American consumerism. All families could gradually build their own home, get their own car, aspire to a weekend home, then get a little boat, and so on.

But the post-war reconstruction was also a common nation-building project, and as such had a social side. It was consumption with an end, viz. that of rebuilding a society. Consumption today is excessive by comparison: it is a consumption mostly built on created needs, which is endlessly being renewed because the market profits from it. The common man and woman today are largely prisoners of market forces. They are tempted to want ever new things, new luxuries. Life is more and more concentrated on acquiring these things. There is no critical distance to the market, which dominates society and our lives far too much.

This kind of materialism makes us appreciate appearances: do I look rich? Do I have the social status that others admire? Am I on a par with my fellows in terms of possessions? Do I feel materially 'on top'?

The less we are mature as human beings, the easier we fall prey to materialism. The things possess and dominate us, not vice versa. Without the things the market tells me I need, I am nothing. The market creates more than new needs, it also creates lifestyles and image, exploring the human being's search for values and meaning. The natural inclination is to ask, 'Who am I?' Today the market tells you, 'You can choose: we sell you an image which is who you are.' The young especially fall for this forgery. It goes with the idea, so common today, that there is nothing else to be found: there is no answer to the question: 'Who am I?'

There is also another kind of materialism which is closely related to the above: the view of the human person as a being made up only of flesh and blood. When the body is weak, sick, or dead, there is nothing left of the *person*.

The body *is* the human being. This materialism is as old as history itself, but seems to me to be very prevalent in our time. It is manifested in the lack of respect for those who are physically 'sub-optimal'; but also in the idolatry of the body; in the debates over abortion and euthanasia, and in the general, but often implicit view of each other as acceptable only when we are physcially strong, young, and attractive.

Abortion has since long been accepted as a procedure after failed contraception, or not even that, simply as a form of contraception. Why bother about this at all? The shock of discovering that one takes human life – and the abortion procedure leaves no doubt about the existence of a small human being – is to be avoided at almost all cost. We will not accept this as unique and human, but only as <u>Materie</u> – as material.

In Norway the aborted foetus is officially named 'abortion material' – 'abortmateriale'. What you can see is what exists; thus, there can be no human being before you can see it. The trouble with abortion is that you can mostly see that what is aborted is a little a human being. Therefore, one must rename it something else, such as 'abortion material'.

The Danish paper *Politiken* reports that a late-term abortion was granted on account of a small medical problem, a cleft palate that can easily be corrected by a simple operation.[1] The child was not perfect, and was therefore killed.

---

[1] 'Abortgrænse i opbrud', *Politiken*, Copenhagen, 7 May 2001.

This is contemporary reality and the consequence of a material view of the human being.

The same 'objectification' – in German *Verdinglichung*, literally 'making into a thing' – is visible in the euthanasia debate. The old and sick are somehow less human than the rest of us. The fact that they are weak and sick reduces their claim to being fully human. When the body is near death, it seems that it is no longer fully entitled to equal treatment as a human being. The political debate on introducing euthanasia is only possible because we have a tremendous distance from those whom we debate. We are not talking about ourselves at all, but about someone with less 'humanness' than us. The material view of the other is the reason why this is possible. It defines humanness as a function of health, age, and success – of *material* appearances.

Others that are endangered by the material view of man today are the poor, the handicapped, and the otherwise marginalised. We don't see them at all, and we secretly think that they are worth less than us because they are weaker. They call for respect, mercy, and real solidarity, but they are somehow excluded from the universe of the successful and the 'normal'.

When one reads the international human rights instruments, one encounters the word 'human dignity' which is the only and the very basis for human rights. What does 'dignity' mean? It is not something one can see and touch, but it is nonetheless a recognisable quality. Every person possesses dignity, says the UN's 'Universal Declaration of Human Rights' of 1948 and all later human rights instruments.

Once when I negotiated in a UN conference for the Holy See, I had a meeting with the Norwegian delegation of the then socialist government. They were very suspicious about my insistence that women have dignity. 'What is that word "dignity",' they said, 'some sort of bourgeois repressiveness?'

Dignity is what makes a human being a person, and it is a completely non-material quality, although the body also has dignity. You show that you recognise the other person's dignity when you respect him, but when you treat him as an object, as a thing, as material, then you deny him this dignity. To show respect is the major indication that you know what dignity is.

Prisoner of the Self

Our time is also marked by an overwhelming degree of subjectivism. If I were to point to one feature of our time which is a problem from the point of view of achieving human happiness, it is precisely this subjectivism.

By this I mean the almost commonsensical presumption that everything revolves around myself; that I, the ego, am the centre of the universe. Contemporary man is unhappy, to the extent that he is wrapped up in himself. He is in many cases a prisoner of this self.

One kind of subjectivism is of course plain, old egoism: I want this, I desire that, I will such and such, and I do it if it pleases me. This is age-old human nature. The difference in contemporary egoism and the traditional variant seems to be that there are few, if at all any, censures against egoism today. Egoism seems OK because there are no alternatives. In previous generations one learnt that it is wrong to be egoistic, but do we learn, or even teach, the same at all today?

Instead we see the display of narcissism all around us: in the media, in politics, in the press: 'Look at me! I own this or that; I am rich'; or: 'Look at me! I am important! I have this or that position' ; or 'Look at me! I am beautiful! I look young, I am successful, I am ahead of you'. This is the message that bombards us all the time. It is not a message of admiration of good virtues – it is not a message that says 'this person is good because he has done this or that'. No, it is all the time the message of a narcissistic society – of vanity and self-love.

Again, this is human nature. We are all tempted to be self-centred; in fact, we are naturally narcissisitic to a great extent unless we fight consciously against it. The problem today is that we don't.

But there is also the very important side to subjectivism that has to do with what the Germans call *Grundbegriffe*, or basic principles. This is a philosophical term, but one which is easy to understand: it means that there are some ordering principles or norms that come before all else and which make it possible for us to know ourselves and the world.

One such principle is for instance that human nature exists and is a universal given – all human beings share in some basic tenets of personhood.

Another is that all human beings can know certain things in life, such as basic good from basic evil. Most people still react with repulsion against evil unless they are totally corrupted, regardless of which culture or religion they belong to.

But today there is a dangerous subjectivism with regard to these *Grundbegriffe*. Some even maintain that nothing exists outside myself, of the subject that I am. Everything is constructed in my image; nothing exists objectively, by itself, independently of me. And even if one cannot deny that a tree or a car exists objectively, one maintains that the meaning of these objects is subjective, viz. that they have a meaning for me only.

Even worse: good and evil are just about personal feelings and subjective views.

Further, my version of reality is not possible to communicate to others; thus, I live in my world, you in yours, and there is no common ground between us. This is reminiscent of the invention called 'virtual reality' whereby a person lives and enters into a world of subjective experiences.

Why is this dangerous? Because it makes us inhuman and irresponsible; amoral and autistic. If my world is my private one that cannot be communicated to others, then there can be no moral norms that are objectively true. In fact, there can be no truth and no measure of truth and lie, of right and wrong. This position implies total relativism, which in turn means that politics and law rest on ever-changing subjective norms. That in turn means that eventually might becomes right, and that justice cannot exist.

Traditionally we speak of ontological realism, or meta-physics, in philosophy. This refers to the position that the world – things and norms – can be known by us, and that they have an existence that is real, viz. objective. It is I, the subject, that discovers these realities, through experience and deductive reasoning. But the reality of human nature and the world is a given.

Against this view there has been a long row of philo-sophical positions, the most famous being the struggle between the realists and the nominalists in the Middle Ages, which largely followed the split of Catholicism and Protestantism at that time. The nominalists said that there can be no knowledge of the essence of things – we know things only because we give them a name – 'nomen'. We can then change the name, and the 'thing' for which the name stood, is no longer there – it does not exist apart from its name. In fact, it is only the name of a thing that we can know, not the thing or the object itself. To take a current example, the word 'family' does not stand for anything real in itself, but only for whatever we choose to call a family.

But today the old nominalism is replaced by a much more radical subjectivism which says that things are out there only to the extent that I, the subject, recognise them. They only exist in my image of them. In such a world there is nothing we can have in common – neither a belief in God, nor common ethics, nor law. The whole concept of law presupposes equality and objective treatment, and that the subjects of the law accept the law as equally valid for all. Then law must refer to universal norms – to the concept of justice as such.

Nothing makes me more worried than this construc-tivism in matters pertaining to the institution of the family and to Christianity. Here the word 'family', that is, what calls itself a family is stereotyped. Anyone living together can be a family. What is exasperating is not so much that the family concept is applied to anyone's arrangements, although this poses problems as well; but more the approach: that there is nothing to be sought that corresponds to the word 'family'. This is a radical nominalism that makes inter-subjective understanding, discussion, and decision-making ultimately impossible. If only subjective views exist, then decision-making becomes the tyranny of the majority.

We see the same approach with regard to Christianity in Scandinavia and in several other western states: Christianity is used to support any position. The contest over the state church in Norway is a dialogue of the deaf: On the one hand, the traditional Lutherans who cling to *sola scriptura* and who arrive at sound theological doctrine based on the word of Christ; on the other hand, some theologians who ridicule them for being traditionalists and backward.

In the latter group, Christianity can be anything: my version of Christianity is as good as yours, and every interpretation about any subject is possible. This is extreme nominalism, and it is far from the faithful theology of traditional Lutheranism.

But if the Church is a people's church, as the slogan goes, then it must mirror all groups in society in order to be democratic, and everyone must find their version of God in the Church so that they can feel at ease there. No one must condemn anything as a sin, because this is contrary to the commandment of love; one continues, and being intolerant is intolerable, whereas, I may add, everything else must be tolerated.

I would think that Christ Himself, and His apostles, were extremely intolerant by these standards. They not only said unpopular things, but they claimed that you would perish forever if you continued to sin. Today such theology is not only backward, but outright intolerable to many. The state church in Norway is going to be what we, the people, vote it to be. If someone tries to tell us that there is an objective reality called truth to be looked for in the Gospels, then that person is reactionary at best. We change Christianity to fit our views, and there is no middle ground.

Then it is however we who make God in our image, and not vice versa.

The above may seem harsh, but it mirrors the reality in the politico-theological debate in many western states. I am disturbed by the theology of this – the tremendous confusion that normal people experience, and which makes them think that Christianity is a political battle-ground and nothing else.

But I am even more disturbed by the approach: that there is no one truth to be looked for and eventually found, but that the normal thing is to make God as you like Him. Perhaps one should name it 'therapeutic theology': it makes you feel good to believe in something. The French revolution banned God and established 'Le grand Etre' instead. This is far more preferable and less danger-ous than God 'a la carte'.

In my own search for something – at the time I did not know what – this was what disturbed me the most. I could never accept that the subject is all that exists, and that there is nothing objective to discover. In short, I could never accept that there is no truth to be discovered.

There had to be truth, and the search for truth must be the ultimate object of study and research. Let me put it this way: if there is no truth about our lives, about our exis-tence, what is there to live for? As you gather, this is the *Leitmotif* of this book, and it is intimately connected with the problem of subjectivism of today.

Useful People

Our time is characterised by utilitarianism. This is the tendency to see other people as things to be used, as objects. When women are represented as sexual objects, they are used, not respected. In interpersonal relations there is a great deal of utilitarianism, viz. the confusion of a person and a thing. A person can never be possessed, but requires respect and has his or her own dignity. A person simply *is* in his uniqueness. A thing is an *object* made to serve us; while persons are never made to be used by others, but to be respected as human beings. A person should receive this respect simply by virtue of being, not by virtue of being useful.

In our time there is to be a very utilitaritian view of people. Love is presented in the media and popular culture as self-satisfaction: I love a person because he pleases my ego. He satisfies my needs. Sexuality is not about self-giving, but about acquiring sexual satisfaction. Thus it becomes a kind of self-love by extension: this or that person reinforces my ego, my view of myself. What passes for love today is in reality very much the opposite; utility.

The same kind of utilitarianism can be seen in professional as well as private relationships. In professional life, networks are the key to success, and this is perhaps just appropriate, but when private friends become friends as a result of calculation, it is wrong. In the family we may find the only place where calculation does not enter: here people are accepted and loved as they are, organically and naturally.

In December 2001 I headed the Holy See's delegation to a UN conference on the commercial sexual exploitation of children in Japan. This kind of gruesome adult abuse of children is really the ultimate utilitarianism. We see it in sexual exploitation of women, and even of children: human beings that can be used for some perverse pleasure can be bought and sold. In such cases we can really talk about using and abusing others. The abuser is totally blind to the dignity and personality of the other human being.

We are rightly shocked by this, but we should watch our tendency to view others as objects in less blatant ways.

It is so easy to keep one's distance.

The lost knowledge of human nature

If our time is characterised by these features I mention –
materialism, subjectivism, and utilitarianism, was it any
better before? And is there really so much wrong with this
anyway? In other words, aren't I constructing a problem
that is not there?

At first glance you may be right. It is wonderful to
satisfy one's needs and desires. That is all very natural.
But there is no lasting happiness in this. The satisfaction is
soon replaced by a feeling of emptiness. There must be
more to life; in fact, there is, I venture to say, another kind
of life that is hidden to the superficial person. That is the
subject of this book.

I think we are really worse off than my parents' generation because then one learnt that there are some common
norms about right and wrong that are authoritative.
Today there is much less agreement on this. Human
nature has not changed, but the correctives to human
nature have largely disappeared. Secularisation accounts
for much of this, as does the fragmentation of society. The
sources of moral authority in society – parents, Churches
and schools – have been weakened, for complex reasons.

Why is egoism bad? Why can't we just accept utilitarianism and materialism? Who am I to moralise about these
matters? If people prefer to be egoists, isn't that their own
choice which should be accepted?

The ultimate answer to this is that it brings no meaning
in life, no happiness. These features of modern society are
in fact obstacles to the good life. I will try to suggest why
this is so. We are made with a longing for happiness, and
we can find this happiness. But it is not a material happiness, in a way it is rather becoming what we already are –
becoming as great as we have been intended to be. There
is a hidden greatness about the human being which we
can make a reality, and this greatness is our image and
likeness to God.

What was it our fathers knew and transmitted to us
about good and bad? Perhaps they never reflected on it,

but everyone 'knew' that there were rules about right and wrong, good and bad. It is bad to envy, to steal, to kill, to think only of oneself; it is good to think of others, be honest and upright, be good to others, respect them, not to be overly materialistic, etc. These were the Ten Commandments transmitted as common rules of ethics. Every parent knew what these rules were, and no one really questioned them. At that time Church and school transmitted the same values. There was a strong common basis of values in western society.

This basis has eroded over the last couple of generations. This has complex causes, not to be discussed here. But it remains a fact that the three instititutions: parents, school, and Church exert much less influence in society than before. There is today a widespread mentality that you can live as you like; that there are no rules at all apart from the idea that tolerance is the only norm.

But often this tolerance is practised quite tyrannically – only what is 'politically correct' and condoned by public opinion is tolerated. That is mostly the old liberal dictum that you can do anything as long as it does not hurt others. But today this is much more radical, for there are no norms left to restrict you.

Others' views are easily labelled 'undemocratic' and 'intolerant', especially the suggestion that there is a truth to be found and ethical norms to be discovered.

There used to be common knowledge of what is traditonally known as *virtues* and *vices* in European philosophy and theology. Virtues are those qualities in a human being that make him good; vices are those that make him bad. The word 'virtue' is derived from the Latin word 'vir'. It means 'manly' in the sence of 'strong'. A virtuous person is a strong person. The traditional curriculum included reading of the classics, where philosophers like Seneca and Cicero discuss how to become a virtuous man. Plato and Aristotle, among others, also have this as the main theme in their ethical and political writings.

The human virtues include fortitude, temperance, justice, and magnanimity, to mention but a few. One should train oneself, like an athlete; to become strong and just, generous and moderate. Corresponding vices include vanity, sensuality, gluttony, pride, and impatience. The goal in life is to become noble as a person, and this is done by combatting the viler tendencies of human nature.

Human nature was known to have both good and bad tendencies, and training was needed all the time in order to succeed in developing the virtues.

In Christianity the human virtues are developed through the specific ethics of Christ's teaching: humility as opposed to pride and vanity; charity as opposed to egoism, and so on. Christianity adds the theological virtues of faith, hope, and charity to the classical virtues.

All this knowledge of human nature and norms was handed down to us through the centuries, and somehow transmitted through the institutions I mentioned. The essential theme was to teach the human being to live a good and right life, and this could only be accomplished by a continuous struggle to become better. The term 'askesis', which we associate with a dry and inhuman life, really means to train, like an athlete.

My point here is simply that no generations before us seem to have thought that human nature is OK as it is – they have always known that it needs redemption, and that hard work is needed to live virtuously. But today we don't even think that there is a universal human nature; no less that there is something useful in the traditional knowledge of virtues and vices. Speaking about virtues only makes sense when there is a common human nature anyway. And finally, even if human nature is admitted to exist, there is not a conviction that virtues and vices are relevant as concepts anymore.

But if you ask whether the vices are prevalent today, what you do find when you look around?

Take *gluttony*, which is the vice of over-indulging in food and drink. Don't we see a tremendous preoccupation with food, to the point where obesity is a major problem in most western states? Anorexia is a another manifestation of this. Take *sensuality*, the vice of being overly-attached to the pleasure of the senses. All around us people are valued solely for their looks. What about *lust*, that very good word for excessive preoccupation with *inter alia* sexuality? This age is 'sexualised' to such an extent that children are deprived of the innocence of childhood by being introduced to sexuality far too early, and adults are almost 'abnormal' if they stay married to the same person for a lifetime and think that sexuality is an expression of deep commitment and love. Take *pride*, the worst vice of all. The opposite is humility, where forgetfulness of self and service to others are the signs. I do not see many humble people around. On the contrary, the ego is the centre of our attention. Take *greed*. Making money is what it's about. Getting more and more is the main goal in life for most people, it seems. Your 'market value' is the most interesting feature about you, that is, how much money you will make or how famous you are.

The 'market value' of a prostitute is an innocent matter compared to the excessive weight put on the 'market value' of the business tycoons.

Thus, a simple run-down of the how the vices fare today gives a lot of food for thought. They seem more relevant than ever. But who today cares to ask himself: Am I greedy, proud, lustful? Or am I generous, magnanious, charitable, humble?

Very few indeed.

This has direct and grave consequences for societal and political life. The 'common good' which is what politics should be about, is a completely antiquated and meaningless term in a society with such values, deaf to the question of 'public virtues'.

The prevalent mentality today is that you, the subject, can choose infinitely. There is nothing that is permanent in your choices. The term 'definitive' or 'permanent' seems a horror. We want all options all the time. Likewise, the terms 'duty', 'virtue', and 'commitment' seem curiously old-fashioned. We have been liberated from them, as we have become liberated from every bond and institution handed down by history.

This gives a tremendous freedom to do what we want, but also a tremendous disorientation: What do we want from life? Even more difficult, what is the purpose and meaning of life? Does the question of meaning make any sense at all?

In the following pages let me share with you what I found, pursuing the quest for meaning in my own life. I will tell you about the quest itself – how I arrived, with many detours and setbacks, at more certitude about the meaning of life, which I – to my tremendous surprise – found in Christ. To find Him there are as many ways as there are persons, but the goal is the same, and the discoveries are the same.

In posing that essential question of happiness, of meaning, one ventures into new territory where one can always choose to go back to the simple and certain road map one had initially. One can always revert to the 'safe' position of saying that I am the stable centre of the universe, and happiness is for me to control my life as much as possible: by fulfilling my material desires, by buying me safety unto death, by planning my life and by following my own will. But if one chooses to leave behind this self-centred and self-controlled life, one must adopt a fundamental openness to otherness – to the possibility that there is a meaning that is very different from this. It is a radical thing, to try to follow Christ. It puts great demands on you.

CHAPTER 2

POSING THE QUESTION

There are many who never pose any question of meaning. It would never occur to them. Life is what presents itself. They are satisfied with the material universe around them, and are in a way 'absorbed' by things – by possessing them and by acquiring them. Material well-being is not enough; it is the quest for more possessions, money, and status that is the real driving force of life. This is also a kind of quest for security from death, which we deny for as long as we can.

How does the question of meaning enter one's life? Why do some ask it, others – it seems the majority – not? I don't know the answer to these questions, and I keep wondering why so many people are uninterested in them when they obviously cannot be really happy with material possessions and the quest for material security. Are they happy with this? Or is it an escape; a substitute, for something else?

What is the question of meaning about? It is an existential question about human life and the point of living it. In the face of death, which is certain to come, why don't we ask this question more often? But who wants to think of death?

Although everyone recognises that death will come also to them – probably in the distant future, we all tend to think – it is almost contrary to human nature to be preoccupied with it. We rightly put it off and suppress the thought of the unknown and the frightening. When we meet death, we flee from it as soon as we can. When someone near us faces death, we try to tell them that it is not coming, that they will get well soon. Death is the ultimate reality we cannot and will not come to terms with. It has no place in our material universe because it means that our bodies will rot and disappear. Who can bear such a thought?

No, the question of meaning will never come out of our fear of death. It is really a quest for happiness. Everyone wants to be happy – the human being naturally seeks to be happy. In order to be happy, meaningfulness is needed somehow. What our lives are about has to be in some way or other meaningful. I think this is the deep driving force behind asking the question. We naturally seek happiness in another person, in family life, in an interesting job, in the ordinary things in life.

How do we find meaning in all this? It depends on our attitude, on our qualities. But it depends first and foremost on our ability to become the human beings we can become. There is something hidden in the human being of which we only catch glimpses in special moments – like when someone helps another spontaneously; when someone is forced by extreme events to let go of all masks; when we cease to act guardedly.

The journey towards meaning must be a journey towards self-knowledge. As a Nordic, I am wont to compare to icebergs: you see only one tenth above water. With the human being, you very often see only the masks and the superficiality, a little, and not the real, part of the human being. There are many more, hidden depths that most people never discover in themselves.

Discovering the European Heritage

I grew up in a small coastal town on the southernmost tip of Norway. It was known for its pious traditions, something akin to what the Americans call 'the Bible belt'. There were sects on each street corner. At the time I did not appreciate what was good and true in this; I regarded these people as backward. They would be puritanical, avid Bible readers, stay together, and bear public witness to their faith. But it seemed smug and overdone and to a great extent it was.

I once joined one of these legion groups for a winter vacation. We stayed at a cabin in the mountains. Each night there was Bible reading, and all of us – apart from myself and another girl – were 'converted', that is, stood up and gave witness to a sudden conversion to the faith. They became 'saved', as it was called. Only I and the other girl stood against this evangelisation attempt. We took off into the woods and sat down by ourselves, using all the swearwords we knew in order to encourage ourselves against this raid on us.

When we came back home, I started to cry in front of my parents. It had been a week's brainwash, but I had not succumbed. The others, the 'newly saved', also left the Christian group after a while.

It certainly was no decent way to evangelise. After that I never set foot in any of the Christian associations in my home town, but entertained suspicion against them. I did not do them justice; laughed at them and ridiculed them. Who did they think they were? Better than the rest of us?

I had long debates about Christ with my aunt, who was a believer, thinking that she was unenlightened and backward, and that this explained her belief. I must have hurt her.

My paternal grandmother, whom I never knew in person, was however one of these Christians. She was a mother of seven, including one retarded child; and she had to be very good at utilising the family income. In addition to all the housework and the daily toil of feeding such a big family, she grew beautiful flowers in the garden, being the town's supplier of flower bouquets.

But she halved her small income from selling flowers, which was so direly needed for herself; always, without any exception, fifty percent went to the 'mission'. If anything was real in the Christian message, such an eloquent example bore witness to it.

The 'mission' was a standard term on the coast. It denoted all the Christian activities aimed at converting the pagans, especially in Africa. There were legion associations devoted to the 'mission' which last to this very day: The 'inner mission', a society aimed at missionary work within Norway, the 'outer mission' aimed at abroad, the China mission, aimed of course at converting the Chinese, and so on. Keeping missionaries alive and helping their work was a major Christian preoccupation. Places like Cameroun and Madagascar were to me closer mentally than the capital, Oslo. Even I was involved in knitting socks for the 'mission' when I was a child. In wintertime we would meet once a week to sew and knit, often with a visiting missionary relating about his work in faraway Africa, showing pictures of happy black children who had become Lutheran.

As an only child, I was both alone and precocious. I solved this by reading a lot. The beautiful library in my home town, an old patrician house from the seventeenth century, had a section for children. It was open twice a week, and one could borrow two books each time. That meant four books per week. I wanted to read more than that. I read widely, also in our home library. This was just before the TV age in Norway, and my parents were also avid readers. Evenings we spent reading. A world was opened to me: of the European classics, of history, of philosophy. I remember reading *The Three Musketeers*, hardly stopping for meals. I loved the gentleman d'Artagnan, not the childish farmer boys in my class.

In school I excelled, not unexpectedly. I liked everything but mathematics, but my ambition to be best made me work hard even at that. I competed against another girl, now my good friend; then the adversary. We were both ambitious and competed throughout the school years.

Nonetheless it was not primarily ambition that drove my work. I had a tremendous love for it, especially all that had to do with history and philosophy; with the European heritage. I don't know where it came from, but it was always there. As a child I had an acute awareness that I was different from most of the others in my class who were interested in normal life in our little town. I knew that I did not want to stay on there, although it made me very sad. I dreaded small town life, and knew from early on that I wanted to get away. That life was about getting married, settling down, having a prosperous, safe and secure life. It was closed in on itself. I don't know why I dreaded it so much, as it was – and is – normal. But I knew inside that there was a world out there and that I was looking for something different. I did not want to settle down and get married.

I liked the things boys did: fishing, boating, rough outdoor things. I took no interest in babies and girls' toys. That was just boring. My hero in childhood was Tarzan, and when my father built me a cabin in a treetop, my happiness was complete. I fished and swam, and sailed in the boat he also built me. I like blunt talk and sporty lifestyles. My professional life has always been with men: in energy, foreign policy, and in academia; in political science.

The childhood in the south was healthy and close to nature. When I visit there with my own family, I relish in the freedom of being at sea, land on remote skerries where only seagulls live; abide on the still surface of the ocean on a long summer night, fishing. The sea and the mountains mean much to me, but the sea most. The people in the small town are the same: practical, simple, knowledgeable about the weather, how to cope in a storm; in short, people who do not know how to play urban sophistication. The Christ I was later to know also had His life among simple fishermen.

Because I was such a clever pupil it was not a problem that I thought about not staying in my beloved home town. 'She has to go to Oslo to study,' they said. And I was content with this escape route.

My childhood was filled with my school work. I pursued it with great love. The long vacations were boring, and I always longed to get back to school. I liked to talk with my teachers, and became their friend.

The teachers also loved their craft – or rather, their vocation. To have teachers that love their work so much is a great inspiration. I learnt German grammar and European history from teachers who truly loved what they taught. Being close to the Continent – only four hours to Denmark by the ferry boat – both we and they would go there for vacations. German and French culture was closer than to the rest of Norway, and we thrived on the old historical lines of contact through shipping and sailing.

In my home area every family had its share of sailors who were familiar with the wider world. Once confirmed – an important religious and family event – a boy went to sea as a sailor. Europe was not a distant place, but part of our history. The 'Dutch period' was in the seventeenth century when sailing ships from my home town would transport timber to Amsterdam – on which the city is built – and bring home exotic fabrics and ceramic tiles. Many a local girl would go to Holland to work, and some came here to stay. We still have the Dutch names – Tønnes, Giert, and Salve – male names you never find in other parts of Norway. Likewise, England was a familiar place, and so was the Baltic coast and Poland.

Nature there was and is the sea. Everything is related to the sea. In winter, there were storms. Sometimes they uprooted trees, and certainly made fishing impossible. The westerly winds were always there, except for some few days in summer. I have heard the wind from the west for as long as I can remember. The North Sea was off the coast, and the southernmost point in Norway, the lighthouse Lindesnes, was close. To pass from the east towards the open sea or along the coast, one had to pass this point. The waves are always very heavy there. I used to sit by the lighthouse to watch the boats disappear down into the valleys made by the waves, for them to reappear on the top of the next wave. At night and in foggy weather, I always heard the long, deep sound of the lighthouse's siren, like a primeval cry from the sea.

The wind, always howling in the autumn and winter, was even personified, as it was the most important variable of life. 'He blows hard today', the locals will say, 'but we will stay him out' – meaning that they would prevail over the wind.

The smell of the sea, carried by the wind, is the freshest scent I know. It is sand, salty seawater, and seaweeds in a mixture served to the sound of shrieking seagulls. That cold water, forever moving, forever new. The sea shows the human being its littleness; the most powerful element of the four, it demands respect. Know the sea, respect the sea, or perish by the sea.

Every year, especially in autumn, many persished. We all knew someone who drowned while at sea. Some were locals whose boat returned home without crew; others were fishermen, a major livelihood even today. My old neighbour, the boy I used to play with, is a fisherman. Fishing was the key livelihood, along with being a sailor. My father, one of seven children with a stern mother, ate fish for breakfast, something he likes to this very day. Cold fish for breakfast, cod's brain for feast days. One such is Christmas Eve, when they all eat cod and especially the delicacy, the brain. Little do they know that this is the old Catholic fast. It is a custom that has survived from Catholic times in Norwegian history.

When I was a child, all this was of course just natural. Were there places where people were not living from, and by, the sea? Were there people who did not know how to sail, or fish? Hardly.

The Joy of Learning

My teachers were a natural continuation of this history and had retained their professional pride in teaching. Learning was for them not only a means to a trade, but an education for the human being. It is the real humanistic tradition that we need to restore, which is ultimately about educating the whole person; about instilling a disposition to virtuous life in a young soul. I loved to speak with them, and I loved the fact that knowledge was an enrich-

ment that opened new horizons to me. They had a tremendous respect for knowledge, and the implicit assumption
was that knowledge cultivated you as a person. This is
nothing less than the European tradition of *Bildung*.

Historically we were closer to Germany than to Latin
countries, while the English influence was strong, too.
From England came the gentlemanly ideal and the
lifestyle, and of course the maritime and trading tradition.
From Germany came philosophy and theology, which
played a great role through Danish dissemination. The
school system was German, as is the Norwegian university system to this day. There was great stress on learning
German.

I loved the literary history and the analysis of characters. This was very much an analysis of virtues and vices –
one could follow a person's life in the books and see how
tragedy happened; or how love was made perfect. One
could see how good prevailed over evil; and how the
drama ended – yes, dramatically.

Today children read so little compared to when I was
young. They get a superficial life of the mind and little
ability to understand the nuances of human life. This is a
danger for them. In my childhood we read a lot, and took
it seriously. It was a necessity to read bits and pieces, at
least, of the European classics. The point of this was not
only to become conversant with these books and authors,
but to learn from them about what constitutes a good and
noble life.

The real subject matter of this was not this or that character in the books, but really virtues and vices, or as they
say in the American movies, the good and the bad guys.
The attraction for us was to recognise good and evil, and
to see if and how good would prevail. We admired the
virtuous persons, and imitated them, in a sense. I did not
see then, only much later, that the attraction of all this was
that it pointed to truth, like images on Plato's wall: There
was something to be discovered through these literary
characters that made them symbols of a larger reality.

None of these teachers had any interest – at least I don't

think so – in Christianity. The latter was a natural part of the curriculum, but was not a particularly important part of it. We had to learn psalms by heart from the first grade onwards – all the magnicent Protestant hymns that came to Norway via Denmark's great psalmist Grundtvig, and before him from reformed Germany. They were mixed with old Norwegian hymns, many of them medieval Catholic.

We learnt at least one psalm per week. I fretted over them by night, but discovered that I knew them the next morning. We also learnt about the Bible – the subject was in fact called 'Bible knowledge'. It was a great education in the history of the faith, but at the time it carried no signficance for me apart from constituting history. I pictured Jesus as a nice young man in a tunic with long hair and a beard. He was kind to everyone, and could be seen in most Norwegian homes as a white porcelain replica statue by the famous Danish sculptor Thorvaldsen. I still have one of these figurines on my bookshelf.

Jesus was the nicest man thinkable; He was almost like a southern fisherman. The Christian women talked about Him as if He were one of their guests for the daily coffee-and-cake. He was cosy, like a mild-mannered and meek local inhabitant. Israel, Judea, and Jesus blended into southern life like natural elements. Jesus belonged in the living rooms, like the geranium plants on the window sill. He was pictured on embroidered wall carpets and paintings, always with the same mild-mannered expression. The southern women were pious, puritanical, and hard-working. The men were quiet and sturdy. They rarely showed any display of temper. It was an austere life.

In school we learnt a good deal about Jesus' life, but very little about the development of the Church. In the books, one went from St Paul to Luther, only mentioning a little about the selling of indulgences: 'Wenn das Geld im Kisten klingt, die Seele in den Himmel springt.'[1] This

---

[1] 'When money comes into the coffer, the soul leaps into heaven.'

verse from the Dominican friar Tetzel, infamous for selling indulgences, was in the book, but apart from that there was little about the Catholic Church. I learnt Tetzel's selling slogan by heart. It must have made a strong impression. He was even pictured, as the only Catholic, in that book, looking devious and cunning.

My years at the gymnasium – up to nineteen – were spent studying. I wanted to go to the university, but did not know which field. History was too backward-looking, languages were tools but I did not want to become a philologist; law was practical and what my parents wanted.

I postponed the choice of study by one year when I received a sholarship from the Norwegian Crown Prince to go to an American college for one year: I stood in the hallway of the gymnasium in my home town Mandal when I caught sight of a small sign inviting applications for this scholarship. I applied and was successful, winning what was called 'tuiton' for a year. Little did I know that it only covered the teaching. My father had to pay the rest.

The US was the closest place for southerners apart from the black Africa of the 'mission', and the North Sea states. In every family someone had emigrated, ending up as floor layers in Brooklyn or as farmers in the Midwest. Those who came back gave their children names like Glenn, Randolph, Stanley, and Gordon – also common names today. 'Over there' was Brooklyn, only a little sea journey to these coast people. The locals used American measures to indicate size: 'That town is half as big and twice as dead as an average American cemetery', they said about a neighbouring town. Everyone understood the comparison.

Before I left for the US that autumn I had spent some summer weeks in Europe, all on my own on the train. My parents were worried about this gypsy-style travel; this time probably with good reason. I wanted to see all the places which figured in European history that were already familiar to me.

I took the boat to Denmark and the train all the way to

Italy. I came to Venice at two a.m., and slept in the moon-light on the pavement next to Canal Grande. The train station is next to the canal: you simply walk outside, and there it is.

Venice was a tremendous city. I bathed in history. After Venice: Florence, Assisi, and then Rome.

I wanted to see St Peter's. Arriving at Stazione Termini, my big rucksack on my back, I boarded one of the old green buses for Via della Conciliazione. There, in the intense summer heat, I saw the cupola and the façade of the church at the end. I can picture it today as it was then: imposing, big, like a layer cake, a dizzying sight in the hot sun. Baroque architecture at its most impressive: I have never liked the style, but St Peter's is, by all measures, a sight.

I stayed in Rome for more than a week, living *gratis* on the roof of the youth hostel at Foro Italico. It was too hot indoors, and I did not have much money.

The meeting with history in this tangible way that Rome presents, was fantastic. There is layer after layer of history that could be studied and even touched. I could have stayed there forever. The fascination with the *tangible* character of history was what fascinated me: I could touch and see what I had only read about. The Romans had lived here and built the city. There was no doubt about it. The Christians had been persecuted here, and hid in the cata-combs. St Peter and St Paul *were* there. I even saw the prison where they had been. Living persons like you and I had been Christians there, only some few years after Christ Himself. They had even died for it. What better evidence could exist that Christianity is more than fiction? I was fascinated.

No one could doubt that these people had been here. It was REAL. There was continuity to this very day: even the most uninformed and doubtful person must accept that there was this continuity. I was extremely happy to discover this, for it confirmed my idea that there is a

European identity and European values. In the north, we have comparatively less history: Viking graves with ships and some Viking houses, almost nothing from the medieval period in terms of churches and monasteries, and the sad interruption in historical consciousness brought by the Reformation.

In Rome I found *continuity*: this is much of where Europe was formed, the main focus of development also for the northern part. To see and *touch* this past, which is also the link with the present, meant very much to me.

But Christian Rome did not attract me beyond the purely historical interest.

Philosophy's Question

In America I studied at Augsburg college in the Midwest. A Lutheran college erected by Norwegian immigrants, it naturally praised its heritage. But here I also met philosophy as a field of study, in the traditional sense of metaphysics. Philosophy does not exist in the Norwegian curriculum except as a university study, and is not introduced to college students.

The questions of philosophy were the ones that really engaged me. Who is man? What is the good life? Is there a deity? Is ontology possible? How does one discover the truth? Is there a truth to discover?

What attracted me most was the question of goodness – of discovering truth. In political philosophy as well as in ethics, this is the question of virtues and vices. What makes a man good and wise? How can ethics be applied to politics? –

I had found the key question that I had been seeking; without knowing that I was seeking anything at all.

It was in philosophy that I could find answers to the question of a deeper logic or reason. I was interested in learning because there was something deeper there, expressed in nobility in human characters in literature and in knowledge about right and wrong. But it was in philosophy that this was discussed in its pure form: is there a truth? How can we know it? Or is it just sense impression, in our imagination?

In the Lutheran college I had a Catholic professor of philosophy who introduced me to this disipline. I took courses in formal logic and classical and medieval philosophy. I read Aristotle, Plato, and Plotinus; Bonaventura, Cusanus, and Thomas Aquinas that year. It was a great year of exploration; of delving into the true sources of European civilisation. I liked metaphysics, which was possible and knowable; but most of all I liked political philosophy, which was about the question of justice. It struck me that Socrates had said most of all that was needed to reflect on in this field in the Platonic dialogues. My English edition, edited by Richard McKeon, on thin, crisp paper, is full of underlinings and comments.

This Catholic professor treated Catholicism as a philosophical system of pure theory. He was not interested in Christianity in ordinary, practical life at all, but of the logical beauty of Thomism and the scholastics. He found the medieval period to be the purest one in terms of ontological order. After this time there was basically a decline in philosophy and in everything else, he thought. He urged me to become a medievalist and suggested that I should study further at a famous Pontifical Insitute of Medieval Studies in Toronto. I ought to become a scholar, he thought; and thus be able to distance myself from the ugliness of the modern world.

But I opted to return to Norway because I was interested in the study of politics, which is, as Aristotle said, the highest *practical* science. I reacted against the escapism of this ivory tower approach, although I also vacillated. I disliked much about the modern world as well, but it was wrong to shut oneself away. I wanted to do, to act; not to live in a world apart.

What to study for my profession? I settled for law, much according to my parents' wishes, although I was really most interested in political philosophy. I returned to Norway and enrolled at Oslo University. The first course of law was in private jurisprudence and commercial law.

I was extremely unhappy about it. What interested me was international law and legal philosophy; which norms govern international society, if any? Does justice relate to law? How is natural law related to Norwegian law? But these questions were old-fashioned. No one took an interest in them. In Scandinavia there is a very positivistic legal tradition, exemplified by the so-called Uppsala school of Axel Hagerstrøm, who in the 30s argued that law has no relation to ethics at all. Law was simply what a majority decided on.

After a summer's study I changed from law to political philosophy; or rather, to the history of ideas or intellectual history. It is better known by its German name, *Ideengeschichte*. This is a hybrid between history proper and philosophy, tracing and analysing the genesis and influence of ideas on society. I specialised in political philosophy with a heavy dose of German historical philosophy. After a year at Oslo where I did nothing but study I returned to the United States on a further scholarship, staying there for another two years. I completed two Master of Arts degrees in political science and modern European history but chose to return to Oslo to write my thesis. I wanted an academic career in Norway and did not dare to go for an American Ph.D. because they were not well thought of at the time in Norway. One thought that a Norwegian degree was better than anything else.

The only 'religious' experience I had during these years in America was when Pope John Paul II was elected in October 1978. Someone Catholic showed me a page in *Time* magazine, saying, 'we have a new pope'. There was a picture of him on the balcony of St Peter's, waving. I thought, 'no concern of mine'.

But ever since I remember that page of *Time* and its exact layout.

At Oslo I continued to study political science, opting to write a *magister* thesis – the precursor of the old and traditional dr.philos. degree, which I was to complete much later. My topic was democratic theory, and its limits: how to constrain the majority principle by the *Rechtsstaatstradition*. It became a study of European corporatism and the growth of the plebiscitarian principle. Only later did I understand that I was really interested in the Catholic principle of subsidiarity. I could not accept the divorce of politics and ethics; that all there is, is the majority principle. Politics must have a nobler and firmer foundation. There must be some principles that majority voting cannot abolish.

All this time I had been intensely interested in finding a philosophical system that was logical and truthful. I could not accept the prevalent subjectivism in academia and in particular the behaviouralism of American political science. I refused to accept that ethics – the writings of the whole tradition from Aristotle onwards, was simply to be relegated to the history of political science. I had many a heated argument about this. Why was political science scientific today but not before? Could and should it imitate natural science?

Underlying this was what I later recognised to be a concern with metaphysics. I insisted that there must be a truth to be found, to be discovered, by science and by study, and that this was the very point of studying. In other words, I argued that natural law was meaningful and that in philosophy, both epistemology and metaphysics were real and valid pursuits today as they had been for some thousand years of western thought.

I simply don't know why the question of truth was so important to me. I could not accept that there was no truth to be sought after; that relativism was all there was. This issue drove my studies, but it was not only academic, it was also personal. I could not accept the prevalent subjectivism on normative issues.

I still did not know what I was looking for, but I knew that I had to find it, whatever it was. In short, I knew that there was something to be found, but not what it was.

In modern thought there are various strands of subjectivism and relativism, some more relativistic than others.

The most radical of those is the so-called social construc-
tivism, whereby all reality is in the eye of the beholder –
the subject – only. On this view there can be no truth that
is inter-subjectively valid and which can be discovered
and known. This type of relativism makes ethics impossible, and also law, which rests on inter-subjectively
recognised norms.

However, at the time I was a student this school of
thought was not yet in vogue. What was problematic for
me was the idea of progress – that the triumph of empirical knowledge in political science made it scientific and
that all the 'normative' political science, viz. the history of
political science and philosophy – was obsolete. The
underlying premise of behaviouralism was of course that
ethical norms, the question of the just and good society,
was unscientific because it was subjectivistic. The notion
that ethics and norms – that the discussion of political
virtues and vices – was simply a matter of subjective opio-
nion is much older, but with the behavioural revolution in
the social sciences these were finally 'freed' of the
European tradition of legal and political philosophy.

In all this academic discussion my deeper concern was,
as stated, with the problem of subjectivism. This was not
only an academic issue, however – very far from it. *It was
the key issue of making sense of life.* All this time I was
seeking some philosophical system that allowed for the
existence of truth as an ontological postulate, and thereby
made epistemology a possibility. There must be something to strive for that would make sense and that would
give meaning to my life in an existential sense.

In my childhood reading I had found something about
this. It was the treatment of the noble in the human being,
of virtuous and vile persons. In literature as well as in classical philosophy there was this portrayal and analysis of
what a virtuous life is. I had admired literary personalities
because they were virtuous, and read love stories that
dealt with noble love – a love that was attractive because
it loved the finest qualities in a person, and which was
selfless, wanting the best for the other. The conflict

between virtue and vice, and the drama about noble sacrifice in human life, had filled my childhood readings.

Now I sought the same in philosophy: there must be truth about the human being that can be both discovered and analysed. There are norms of good and bad, of justice, which should bear on politics and life for the individual. We as persons must and can improve, and we can learn. If all is relative and mere opinion, then there is no point in studying at all.

This concern of mine continued to haunt me. But I realised that I must be a good political scientist in the empirical sense, because in Norway there was no tradition of, less an interest in, political philosophy in the classical sense. So I qualified in the empirical sense and became an international politics expert, yet my first love – as one says – remained philosophy.

These were my *Lehrjahre* as well as my *Wanderjahre* – I travelled and I studied. But it was all in a certain sense very theoretical. I was still very different from my peers. I was a lone wolf, disciplined in study but with an ambition to read everything relevant. But I was somehow removed from life itself, and lived in my academic world. I had no real interest in becoming integrated in society, and took myself far too seriously. I lived by the books, and in the books.

From reason to some sort of faith

I had heard about a Catholic priest in Oslo – a French Dominican – who had directed the translation of the *Summa theologicæ* by St Thomas Aquinas into French. He was reputedly a very sharp fellow, an expert on Thomism. I toyed with the idea of calling him. I had become interested in Catholicism as a philosophical system, and regarded myself as a Thomist, albeit a rather incompetent one. Should I dare to call this man?

I remember that I sat in an office where I worked, to earn some money for my studies. I looked up the

Dominican house in the phone book. It was in 1980. I dialled the number, but hung up. I couldn't call some complete stranger and tell him that I was a Thomist, too. It was too wild.

After much fretting I did however call. He answered in a business-like tone with a strong French accent. I explained that I would like to meet him because I regarded Thomism as the superior philosophical system, but that I was not at all interested in the Catholic faith. The priest simply told me to meet him later that week. He seemed not the least surprised by my request.

I don't recall any distinct meetings with this Dominican; only that we met every week for a year and half. We read Thomas but also other philosophical works. Gradually these sessions turned into intellectual exercises on the Catholic faith – how could one separate theology and philosophy in Thomas? Of course one could not.

The Dominican liked these discussions as well. I was like a favourite student who shared his love of philosophy. His approach to Catholicism was extremely rational, in the French sense of the term. He had been taught by the great masters, by people like Yves Congar and his like. It was for me a wonderful world of reason and logic. All of Europe's philosophical history was laid out before me.

At this time I was also attracted by the liturgy of the Mass. I went regularly, but was not conscious of any interest in Christianity as a faith. After all, I had always seen the Christians as rather backward and naive. But in this Catholic milieu I discovered that I could have a perfectly rational and intellectual approach to Christianity. There were many academics in this milieu. But I was not interested in a personal sense, I assured myself.

At one of our philosophical sessions, after more than a year's meetings, the Dominican asked me if I planned to become a Catholic. I said no; I am not interested in that, I am an agnostic. I do not believe; but I agree with the rational system of philosopy of Thomas. That's all.

But his question unsettled me. I had seen him for much more than a year. It could not continue for ever.

I thought a lot about what to do. Why not just leave things as they were? I was not a Christian and would never be one – I liked the liturgy and the music, the culture of Catholicism, and the ethical system. But become a Catholic?

The thought was appalling. I wanted my freedom. Why had this priest asked me that question, and why didn't it leave me in peace?

Then I realised, or rather it dawned on me, without logical reason, without analysis – that it was all about a person named Christ. I remember this realisation: I sat with the Dominican in the cloister gardens, an August evening in 1981. I told him that this person Christ had come onto the scene; mysteriously. I had not given much thought to Him before. I never prayed, and I hardly lived – outside the books. But then this disturbing thing had happened, viz. that I was made to see that Catholicism was not a beautical philosophical system – the metaphysics I had sought for so long – but about a *person* who claimed to be as alive today as two thousand years ago. I felt frankly uneasy at this new insight, because it was not rational or logical, but an experience of something personal. I had no reason that could explain this, but I knew that this was the overriding, then only really important question: Christ Himself. He made Himself present in the sense that I suddenly became interested in Him and His life. I did not like it at all. I had not asked for this; I had looked for a rather abstract and logical meaning of life.

Christ, however, recurred more and more in my life. I kept wondering about Him. Could it at all be true, what the Christians believed? I had never studied the life of Christ apart from the sweet stories from my school days, but now Christ was more like a flame that lit up in me from time to time. He attracted me in a non-intellectual sense, as a source of something I did not know at all. It was something entirely new to me, a different kind of joy from what I knew. I did not know Him at all then. The mild-mannered Christ of my childhood has never been a candidate for the meaning of life.

After this realisation a new stage started. It was no longer a question of reading and concluding based on studies; it was also a matter of believing. It was at once easier and more difficult. It became an existential matter, not an intellectual one. And I was good at the intellectual business, but far from mature as a person. But I was, without realising it, falling in love with the Church.

People who are newly received into the Church usually display all the signs of someone in love. It seems strange to an outsider, but it is an empirical fact. They talk about the Church to everyone; they read Catholic books on spirituality, and think themselves at least halfway to sainthood already. They are experts in Catholicism, and they can talk of nothing else. It is enamoration, and it is like the springtimes of the feelings; a lovely time of life.

I was starting to enter this stage myself. I told myself that I had no interest in becoming a Christian – after all, the ones I had so disliked and ridiculed in my hometown were also Christians – but I was drawn to the liturgy even more. I looked forward to the Sunday Mass, started to read conversion stories, and became interested in mystical writers. Around this time I acquired the major works by St John of the Cross and St Teresa of Avila and set out to read them; ambitious as I was. But of course I was light years from understanding anything. When I revisited those works with considerably more maturity many years later, I saw how hopelessly 'young' I was then, also in spiritual terms.

The question of conversion continued to revisit me. I resisted the thought, yet was drawn to it. My Dominican friend asked me: 'What about Easter? It is only some months away.' I already loved the Church, but it was one thing to steal into Mass; quite another to publicly proclaim one's new faith. Did I really believe in anything? Wasn't it all just a fascination?

The knowledge of the negative reactions to a conversion also held me back. My parents certainly, but also my fellow students and friends and the whole anti-Catholic sentiment of Norway. Catholics were still regarded as strange and 'un-Norwegian' papists, like in the UK. They were outside society, loyal to Rome, and not really dependable. Counter-Reformation prejudices still existed.

Beyond Subjectivism

One decisive discovery was noted in the diary which I kept at the time. That discovery was a Copernican point. It changed everything. I wrote down that 'today I realised that there is objective reality in the host after the consecration regardless of what I think about it; of whether I believe in it or not'. I had underlined the last sentence: 'regardless of whether I believe in it or not'. What is referred to by Catholics as the 'real presence' is the belief that Christ becomes present, in reality, in the host and wine, which is consecrated by the priest to become the body and blood of Christ. This is the supreme mystery of the faith; the centre of the Mass, and the key to the Catholic faith in the sacraments.

At the time I had not understood much of this at all, but I grasped the absolutely essential point; viz. that there is a reality outside of me, the subject. This reality is not created in my imagination, but exists totally independently of me. This was for me a breathtaking realisation which decided the whole matter once I understood it: I had looked for a real meaning of life outside me, a meaning that existed by itself and which would give meaning to me in turn. I had looked for metaphysics, for the Goodness of ancient philosophy, for a firm foundation of the virtues, for an affirmation that beauty and goodness, justice and ethics can exist. Now I found that the *ontological reality I had been seeking was in God*, and that God existed in a way that no one could fully grasp, yet in a reality so close by: in a piece of bread. Luckily I was not the centre of the universe, confined to myself; but I was related to God who existed objectively and really outside myself. This was the happiest discovery of my life – there was an order, a plan, and a meaning beyond my limited self.

Naturally this mystery can never be fully understood

or explained. But one realises that it is true in a mystical, veiled way; and one penetrates it more deeply as one becomes more of a Christian. For me this was the tremendous turning point, for I lived in an environment totally at odds with what philosophers call ontological realism – the position that truth exists and can be found. For me this was the essence of education and research: unless truth were a meaningful concept – which means that truth must exist, be real, what was the point of it all? Truth, if it is not man-made and thus subjective; had to be God-made, and thus God had to be the ultimate author of truth. *Finding truth meant finding God – He was truth.* But what was the revolutionary news for me was the discovery that truth in fact existed, apart from me and my subjective views on it.

This insight about the real presence of Christ in the consecrated host was of course not something one found out by learning or logical deduction. Neither was it something one learnt by studying Catholic catechesis. It was simply a gift of grace to understand that this was true, but that gift was only receivable in prepared soil. My search – that I had posed the question – was probably a precondition for receiving this gift, although I shall never know. Each person's way is different. But the 'empirical proof' of something important in the Mass was the repeated longing on my part to return to it: it was not because of the liturgy, the sermon, or the music – all of which was nice – but because of something else, a presence that drew me back each time. I strayed away, I did not care to go to Mass, and I 'forgot' about it. But after each such 'detour' I returned when I felt the emptiness of the lonely self. In front of the Tabernacle – where the consecrated host is kept in the church – I realised that the real love and meaning were hidden, mysteriously, there. After a while I cherished the Sunday Mass so much that I started to long for it during the week. I did not dare to tell anyone about such a strange thing, but went alone there like someone who secretly meets the beloved.

One never understands this mystery of the real presence, but one feels its real effects. There is a presence in the church for those who want to experience it.

My Copernican point was so revolutionary to me because this meant that reality was not my invention. The problem of realism vs. nominalism has persisted in the Scandinavian countries since the Reformation, and it has major, deep, and fundamental implications. If everything is subjective, there can be no moral norms, no truth, and no God. Christianity then becomes therapy.

The Leap

In late 1981 I wrote a letter to the Pontifical Household of the Holy See in Rome. I explained that I contempated becoming a Catholic, but before I decided on that I would like to meet the Pope. It was a blunt and direct letter. I never thought I would receive a reply. But shortly thereafter a friendly, yet very formal letter arrived at my student residence. The prefect of the papal household told me that 'every effort would be made to fulfil my wish'. I must tell them when and where I would stay in Rome.

I was surprised and excited. I went to Rome with my parents; a vacation. They were totally opposed to any conversion – wasn't the Norwegian Lutheran Church good enough, if I insisted on being a Christian? Why stick out and be different from other normal people? Then, why on earth be a Catholic, hardly a social advantage? Catholicism means strange foreign things, like nuns, celibacy, even Mass duty on Sunday, and Catholics are unable to compromise on issues like abortion. Why can't I just 'find God in nature', as Norwegians are wont to; and be content with that? – Must I have such an extreme view on abortion? One cannot have absolute principles in a modern democracy.

The discussion about this has died down over the years, and we have a kind of truce. They are good Christians without knowing it, I would say. They are really good people in the sense of human virtue. I owe them almost everything.

They came with me to the general audience in Rome that Wednesday in 1981 – I think it was 2 December. We sat in the first row in the large *aula*. The Pope came to greet us all. He shook our hands, asking 'Norway?' We said something in German, I don't remember what.

He made a great, loving impression – something ineffable that made us wildly happy, really uplifted for a long time afterwards. My mother, an agnostic and still intensely sceptical about Catholicism, felt it, too. On the pictures from that audience she looks happier than at any other time. She loved the Pope after this meeting. She has the pictures on display today, over twenty years later.

So I converted that Easter. It was 1982; I was twenty-five. I did not really believe or even internally accept all that the Catholic Church stood for, but I had doubted for such a long time that I knew one thing: that I somehow, mysteriously, belonged in the Church.

I was drawn to it again and again, yet hesitated. Couldn't I just remain an onlooker? No one around me was much in favour of this choice, counting my parents, relatives, and friends. But I already loved the Church. I read everything about her – readings that I had no ability to understand. I talked about the Church to everyone given the slightest occasion, and returned to the Mass as often as I could.

It was the love – the being in love – that made me finally convert; not any rational decision. I had gone from reason to faith; or at least to some faith. My faith was not worth much then, but I was in love with the Church. Where this love came from, I did not know. But I was unhappy if I deleted the Church from my life. I loved in a new and different way.

I received my confirmation and first communion from the Dominican priest during Holy Week. There were some friends who came to the Mass when I was received into the Church; not many. I felt lonely and sad. I was dressed up in my festive national costume, but none of my loved ones were there with me. It was a dreary, rainy day.

I went home after that first Mass, thinking 'Now I am a Catholic. It does not feel any different.'

CHAPTER 3

FAITH VS. LIFE

After my official conversion at Easter 1982 it seemed that nothing had changed very much. I went to the Dominican church each Sunday, lived at the student home in Oslo and continued to read, read, and read. I studied European *Geistesgeschichte* and political philosophy. Being Catholic was something none of my co-students was interested in, and I kept it to myself. As of yet I had no notion that this should imply any kind of apostolic activity for myself. Being a Christian was an entirely private matter.

By this time I had met a Hungarian medical doctor whom I was later to marry. In fact, I noticed him when he received communion. It was really strange to meet like that and it was even stranger to find a Catholic husband who shared my European identity in Norway. I never thought I would marry anyway, and had no interest in having children. And I had little hope of meeting someone 'like' me, who shared the same deeper values.

We were married in St Peter's in Rome in 1985 by a good friend, a Hungarian Benedictine, and had four children in rapid succession. Becoming a mother was a revolutionary experience. I had never thought that being pregnant and giving birth could be such a participation in creation. But it is, and can hardly be communicated to others who have not experienced it. The newborn is a miracle of all miracles, and motherhood changes a woman. Anthropology and Christianity meet in childbirth in a way so strong and tangible that no other human experience compares to it.

European Catholicism: The Hungarian Experience

I moved into an atmosphere of Central-European Catholicism which interested me very much: cultured, civilised, much steeped in Benedictine spirituality. But it was totally different from my Scandinavian everyday life, and there seemed to be no bridges to that world.

These years were taken up by pregnancies, childbirth, and breast-feeding, while I wrote my doctoral thesis and worked in the Norwegian Institute of International Affairs. Having children was a blessing; a new world which bristled with the real meaning of life.

My Catholic life was still a 'private' one which no one had any right to know anything about. It had nothing to do with my work or with Norway – we were strangers as Catholics, my husband even more than myself.

But during those years I developed a friendship with the Benedictines, and became thoroughly familiar with Communist Hungary. This was the theatre of good vs. evil, and one in which vices were displayed against virtues. With hindsight I see how important this was for my own development as a Christian.

My husband represented Central European culture in all its traditional aspects. The son of a general who had led the Hungarian army on the Eastern front in the battle of the Don in 1943, he was a refuge who left in 1956 after a childhood of trauma. His father was deported, along with the family, because he was a 'class enemy' under the Stalinist system. The family had lost everything, going from the privileged status of aristocrats to becoming poor among the poorest in a faraway village on the *puszta*. My husband was a little boy when the family first fled from the advancing Russian troops into Hungary, in 1944; and an adolescent when he had to suffer the punishment of the Stalinist system of class change: those on top would be those at the bottom, and the children of the aristocrats and the bourgeouise would not be allowed education, only manual labour. Thus, they would become the proletariat, and stay as such.

My husband had to dig roads and wear the uniform of the 'worker soldiers', those that came from the former ruling class, but who now would do the meanest jobs. His father, a very principled man with much integrity, never succumbed to Communist terrorism. He continued to wear his riding boots every day, and earnt a little giving private lessons in German, French, and English. He also knew Russian from his five years as a prisoner of war in Siberia during the First World War, when he was captured as a young lieutenant. But Russian was not much in demand.

Eventually he was tortured to death by the local Communists in 1961. My husband never saw him again after he fled in 1956.

This family history contains much of the Central European tragedy of the Second World War. For me much was familiar from my studies of European history, but I had never encountered this 'live': A father-in-law who swore an oath of loyalty to emperor Franz Joseph and studied in the monarchy's cadet school in Vienna; who spent five years in Siberia and whose diaries of those years there that were much later sent to us by the Swedish Red Cross who had worked among POWs there; who fled, like the family von Trapp in *The Sound of Music*, to escape the Russians and to be captured by the Americans in Salzburg, where my husband saw a black man for the first time, chewing gum and eating corned beef. Then the tragedy of the return to Hungary, after the father had been in an American camp with people like Messerschmidt and other names we only read about. In Hungary, a trial against him by the Communists on charges of anti-Semitism, but the witness that came forward and had him freed was his good friend the rabbi.

Central Europe under Communism

The long years of repression and oblivion. People were always afraid: at school, that you would be reported on by informers; if you went to Mass, that you would lose your job; if you talked about it, that they would come in the night for you. My husband and his sister were in primary school at this time. They were known as 'class enemies' and no one in the village was supposed to play with them. They were the 'fascist' general's children.

The children were naturally very disturbed by such a childhood. They were estranged in their own country, and even more so in a new one. They both came to Norway because they could study there; my husband choosing medicine as he could not become a musician as he had wanted to. In Hungary it had been the Catholic Church which 'saved' them. Most of the education until the Communists took over was conducted by the various religious Orders. As my husband's family knew both Jesuits and Benedictines, the children were given free places in their schools. The communist government had abolished almost all Catholic schools and religious Orders, effectively suppressing them. But they allowed some very few to remain open, mostly because they needed a showcase to the West: 'Look, we are not totalitarian!'

One such school was the magnificent Benedictine abbey of Pannonhalma in West Hungary; a thousand years old. My husband got a free place there because his mother knew the abbot. It was a risky business, but he was able to live there for four years in the boarding school. The abbott, Norbert Legany, a man of tremendous principle, was called in for police questioning every fortnight and beaten severely. He never complained.

When the 1956 uprising came, my husband was in the uniform of a worker-soldier near the Ukrainian border, doing manual labour as a punishment for his 'bourgeois' background. He fled from the camp, in the north-eastern Hungarian town of Miscolc, and joined those fighting the revolution in Budapest in late October. When the Russians invaded Hungary on 4 November, he fled the country.

It took three weeks to traverse the country to get to the Austrian border. Some farmers gave him some civilian clothes, and finally he came to his old school Pannonhalma, asking the monks to help him across the border to Austria. His old teacher did so, showing him where to cross along the railroad lines in the company of some other former students. The border guards had mined the area, and patrolled with dogs and floodlights from the watch towers. The refugees hid in the train station all day. When darkness fell, they set out. They all managed to reach the Austrian side that night, but many others did not.

Afterwards the special police came to interrogate the monks. My husband's teacher was so badly beaten that he was unconscious before the police car had passed through the monastery gate. When he died years later, the wounds he received at that time were a major cause.

Now this kind of European history is a drama that touches one deeply, not only personally, but as a Christian. Good seemed pitched against evil. No one has analysed the communist system better than John Paul II, knowing it from personal experience. In the encyclical *Centesimus annus* he aptly analyses this political system which he himself did so much to topple. For good reason, the KGB regarded him as a dangerous enemy.

The Hungarian Church held out against a barbarian system which was based on fear and repression. As I write this, I am sitting in a hotel room in Sopron in West Hungary, near the town where my husband fled across the border. His childhood experience made him extremely determined never to compromise with that system, to the point of refusing to go back to his home country until there was a democratic system in place – in 1990.

The personal stories of those who lived under Communism are tragedies. They were denied normal life and development, and they will never get rid of the fear and the suspicion that 'someone is after' them. I have always maintained that the main difference between tyrannies and democracies is the rule of law – that you and I have objective rights that we can claim in the face of power vested in weapons and systems. Fear is when you are unsure of this; fear is when someone can lock you up at will, when you can 'disappear'. Fear is when you have to anticipate the behaviour of the powerful to exercise self-censorship in order to accomodate them. You avoid talking or writing about certain themes; you even deny obvious truths. The communist system was based on the cultivation of fear. My husband did not return because he disdained the power-holders and would never conde-scend to ask them for a visa – although they tried hard to make him return – but he was also unsure of whether he could be arrested. His Norwegian citizenship would stand against his Hungarian, which he has never renounced.

Christ in Hungary

Because of this connection with Hungary I went there myself; the first time as a student in 1981. I was fascinated by the states east of the Iron Curtain, especially from the point of view of political science. The western democracies were all 'polished', that is, all needs were met and most problems are luxury problems. This is as true today as then, and this is why the Balkan states are closer to my heart than any others in Europe. There is a need to do everything: to cultivate good and to get beyond power vested in weapons to power vested in law and democracy. The quest for the point of no return in this process has always intrigued me immensely: when is power really and irrevocably vested in law? We have not reached that point yet in Bosnia, and not at all in other Balkan states, with the exception of Croatia – for the time being.

But politics do not exist in an anthropological vacuum. It has everything to do with the view of the human being that is prevalent in a society.

Hungary in the beginning of the 80s was still a commu-nist, totalitarian state. When one came by train from Vienna, reaching the cross border point at Hegyeshalom, unpleasant police men entered the train with German shepherd dogs. They interrogated all the passengers: What are you doing in Hungary? Where are you staying?

They were brutal, unfriendly, searching under the seats, in the toilets, and under the train itself. Upon leaving, the search was of course much more detailed.

A man I knew, a dentist, fled Hungary in the late 70s. In order to practise abroad he had to bring his examination records and diploma. He was extremely nervous, knowing that if caught he would face imprisonment for many years and a permanent loss of work. His family would be punished, too. He decided to take the risk, for life in Hungary was hopeless, even at that time when the Stalinist period was over.

He was given a visa to visit Vienna for some plausible reason. But at Hegyeshalom the search of the train was long and detailed. He started to sweat, and thought that his diploma would dissolve; he had taped it to his chest as it was so big that it could not easily be concealed. But as his nervousness grew, so did the risk of disclosure.

Luckily someone else attracted the guards' attention. It was a farmer who brought a whole pig with him. The guards told him that it was illegal, and confiscated the animal – no doubt to eat it themselves. But the poor farmer made so much protestation that my friend was left alone.

Such events are only some years back. We tend to forget that the communist system dominated and destroyed people's lives for half a century. Now the only gospel is capitalism. As I write this, at Easter 2000 in Hungary, the only thing that matters here is money. How you get it, is uninteresting. Every man for himself. There is no solidarity at all; only the harshest kind of Victorian capitalism. The rich display their money in tasteless houses and cars, and a lot of conspicuous consumption is everywhere in sight. The cost of a designer T-shirt equals the pension of an old person who has worked all his life. The middle class has disappeared by becoming poorer and poorer with inflation. They can just afford to eat and live very modestly. The retired people are worst off – some of them depend on soup kitchens. It seems that getting rid of communism has led to the worst excesses of capitalism. Foreign capital owns the country, and the Hungarians are subject to a new kind of colonialism – the economic one.

What these contrasts offer, is a view of how materialism works. Communist materialism was one of a denial of the spiritual aspects of human nature. Man was just a number in a mass – no individualism, no rights, no choice. Capitalism offers another kind of materialism – you are what you consume. Everything centres on buying and using; not on being. Under Communism the Church played a role as a spiritual haven, despite being persecuted severly. Today there seems to be a total indifference to the Church.

My Hungarian life had a lot to do with my Catholic formation. I went on my own to Hungary for almost ten years before the fall of the Iron Curtain. There I met Christians who had absolutely nothing but a strong faith, and that made an indelible impression on me. These people were so well-educated and cultivated in the traditional sense of the term. They knew that human life was about fostering virtue and fighting vice, and they had the whole classical curriculum to draw on. The schools had remained scholastically good throughout Communism, although certain subjects were impossible to teach honestly, such as history. But people read literature, and kept a tradition alive that way. In the homes no one believed in the official 'newsspeak'.

Principles vs. Conformity

On my first trip to Hungary I went with a student friend, Vera. We were both adventurous women, taking off without many plans. Upon arriving in Budapest, we took a taxi far into the countryside to visit a famous national figure, Deszo Kerestury. I knew about him and his writings and political activity – which was all banned – but he of course did not know about us. But we had found the address of his tiny wine yard, and the taxi driver finally located the place.

The welcome was characteristic of Hungarians. They want conversation, good food and drink. Vera and I sat for hours in the garden talking in German with this erudite eighty-year-old in the forty degree summer temperature. The consumption of plum brandy and strong cigarettes was compulsory. The conversation was great – about European history, culture, politics – fantastic. This type of intellectual does not exist any more. And Christianity was of course an integral part of it.

When we parted both Vera and I were aware that we had met a great mind. I wrote a long article about him in the Norwegian press, but I don't think anyone understood what it was about.

The only other thing I remember distinctly from that trip was the Baroque church by the Danube in Budapest. We went there, and found a young priest. He spoke some German, but was greatly embarrassed when I started to ask him whether he was persecuted by the regime. Poor fellow, I had forgotten that it was dangerous to talk to foreigners. The last thing he wanted was to speak with us. He must have cursed these inquisitve women.

After a week in which we had tried to use up our money on food and taxis, without total success, we headed back on the train. The smell of communist car fuel was distinctive – I have smelt it so often that I almost miss it – and of the awfully strong cigarettes, worse than Gauloises, which I had trained myself to smoke while on inter-rail in my teens.

But we almost went to jail instead of to Austria. On the border crossing we realised that we had forgotten to register with the police. This was a must until 1990. You had to go to a police station and fill in a long form about where you would spend the night. If you failed to do this, you could be arrested. Both Vera and I had forgotten this, and since we were still stupid and immature, we started to giggle when the policeman inquired. We should have prostrated ourselves instead, and offered him a bribe. So we can count ourselves lucky that we got out. He was not amused.

What interested me so much about the Hungarians was not their political experience itself. Power concentration and tyranny are not unusual or new phenomena in the world. But what was so intriguing was the fact that these people lived for something else. They really appreciated culture and the classical tradition. Maybe they did this because there was nothing else by way of material goods or political and societial stimulation. I don't think this is the explanation, however. The Hungarians that I knew were middle class and thus educated, and this was still a very clearly class-divided society. But what I liked so much was their real interest in European values and culture. True, they were dreamers – there is even a word for that, 'delibab', which means someone who never puts things into practice. But they had a true respect for history and loved to debate ideas that derived from the great tradition of European thinkers. The contrast to Scandinavian pragmatism was total.

Christian values and norms were a natural part of this – No one debated the *Grundbegriffe*: the point of education was to acquire virtues and fight vices. One read the classics in order to learn from them and to integrate their wisdom in one's own life. The curriculum in the schools had curiously managed to retain much of this, perhaps because the Communist *nomenklatura* wanted the best education for their children and sent them to the few remaining Catholic schools. The hypocracy was total, and everyone knew it. To be a Communist was just a way of social advancement and upward mobility. That explains why those who did not conform regarded the others as traitors and opportunists, which they truly were.

The Communist regime suppressed the Church, and it never enjoyed the role that it had in Poland. After all, Catholicism was the religion of the Habsburg empire, while Calivinism was the truly Hungarian national religion of those who made the uprising in 1848, led by the legendary Kossuth Lajos, who was caught and beheaded by the Austrians. But during the communist era the Prostestants were much easier to suppress than the Catholics because of the lack of an international seat or headquarters. The See of Rome proved, as before in history, extremely important because it could not be suppressed.

The Catholic Church I became acquainted with in Hungary from 1981 onwards was thus a Church that showed resilience and traditionalism. Stripped of almost all its property, its schools, which numbered thousands, closed; its clergy expelled and Orders abolished; it nonetheless exercised influence through the knowledge people had of it. There was a natural respect in those who had known the Church, but the younger generation which grew up in the communist universe naturally did not know anything about this.

In Hungary I was to lucky to be exposed to how Christianity traditionally was integrated in European culture. The same can – or should one say, could? – be found in Spain, Austria, Italy, and Poland. Christianity was taken for granted in these cultures. Today this is no longer so, and we cannot and should not restore what once was. The clericalism of Hungary was appalling, and still is, and no one would want that back. The Church was also very much part of the class structure which perpetuated the aristocracy, the bourgeoisie, and the feudal system, which lasted until 1945. The great Orders – Benedictines, Cistercians, and Augustinians – owned and lived from the land. They were landlords for centuries, and could cultivate scholarship and learning because they were rich.

This was an integral part of a society which had a class of landowners who owned most of the country, and who dominated culture and the arts. The lesser aristocracy and the bourgeoisie sent their children to the best Catholic schools, and the clergy were sought after for their teaching ability. This classical education and erudition was important socially, akin to the British ideal of the gentleman. Manners and refinement were necessary in order to move at ease in the higher social classes. In this system the workers were and remained workers – they had little chance of upward mobility. Thus, the Stalinist model of turning society upside down by denying education to the sons of the higher classes was very efficient in destroying the old order.

I came from an extremely egalitarian society in Norway, where almost all of us came from some small place where we lived simply and very democratically. Thus, I have never had any respect for class or rank, and despise the snobbery that goes with this. The class society I met in Hungary I did not like, and found the clericalism of many of the bishops rather disgusting. They lived in a 'natural' social class with certain privileges, and had never reflected on this. One wonders whether Christ would feel at home in this setting.

Once I visited the bishop's palace in the town of Szombatheley, where my father-in-law had been the regional commander. The bishop showed us the murals on the walls, stopping in front of one with a woman, curiously listening to someone's conversation. 'Hier sieht man die weibliche Neugierichkeit', he said seriously, factually – 'here the female curiousity is portrayed'.

Pannonhalma

But there was an authentic Christianity amidst all this, and I found it in Benedictine spirituality. In 1983, at Easter, I went to the abbey of Pannonhalma, a thousand years old, situated on the Martinsberg where St Martin of Tours was reputed to have been born. I went alone, but as a kind of special envoy of my husband; as this was his old school and he wanted me to visit the abbot before it was too late.

I was in Austria, and traversed the border like several times before. It was Easter Day. In Györ, the town nearest to the abbey, I stopped to change trains. This was also where all my troubles began.

I had been told that everyone spoke German. That was, however, before the Second World War. If anyone spoke a foreign language now, it was Russian. I was stranded, because I spoke neither Russian nor much Hungarian. The few words I knew were some useful phrases of politeness and some very bad swear words, which would turn out to come in handy as well.

Then I had been told that there was a train to the abbey – all proper abbeys are, as you may know, on hill tops in vast pastoral landscapes. This one was no exception – one could see the magnificent buildings, from Romanesque to Baroque architecture, from far away. The rest of the landscape was flat, making the abbey's imposing silhouette even more spectacular.

But there was no train. I inquired in the ticket office, where I was brusquely rejected by a firm lady who spoke only Hungarian. I tried again, in German, but to no avail. The answer was a definitive 'nincs' – 'there is none'. Finally she pointed to a dirty timetable, indicating a local train late in the afternoon, accompanied by a lot of talk of which I understood nothing. So I bought a ticket for that train. What else could I do?

By this time I had attracted so much attention in the train station that there was a crowd discussing me. I looked like someone from another world: tall, with a hat and an elegant Austrian Loden cape. I carried one of those old doctor's cases, filled with bottles of Benedictine liqueur (what else to give a Benedictine?) and forbidden literature in Hungarian. The latter was a gift from a Benedictine living in Austria. When he heard that I was going to Pannonhalma, he insisted that I bring books about the famous – or infamous – Hungarian Cardinal Mindszenty, who had stayed in the US embassy in Budapest until 1972, protesting against the Russians. His cause was noble enough, perhaps, but finally he was overtaken by events when the Holy See initiated dialogue with the East. Mindszenty felt betrayed. He lived the rest of his life in Vienna, but had remained a sort of symbol of the resistance of the Church to Communism. He was a prince of the Church in the old clerical sense. When he went to a friend of mine who is a dentist, he said: '*Unser* Zahn tut weh', employing the royal 'we' even then.

So I should have refused to carry those books; they

were superceded by events anyway. I started to sweat, thinking about what would befall me if they were found. How stupid can you get? To break the law intentionally in a hostile place is ridiculous. I contemplated throwing them in the waste basket, but I was being observed all the time. One man who had had too much to drink followed me around. I shouted at him in foreign languages, angrily, but he had staying power. Finally I used some of the emergency swearing I knew in Hungarian, and when I referred to the less noble parts of the stallion, he looked impressed and disappeared. Hungarian has more bad swearing than any other language I know, but also more ways of politely addressing a person according to his or her rank.

So I resolved to go about the next important task, which was to register with the police. Again I suffered from the language problem. Where was the police station? I walked around, asking in German. To no avail. Why should one talk to foreigners? Finally I went into a hotel reception where they spoke German. They wanted me to change some hard currency in return for helping me out, which I did, and armed with a piece of paper which said 'Rendörseg'; I went ahead again, dragging my heavy luggage and looking very Austrian and bourgeouis.

After asking three times and traversing a bridge, I found the police station in a back yard. The interior was, like all unfriendly police stations in undemocratic states, painted in green, lit by a bright neon light. There was no enthusiasm for my request to register when they heard where I was going. I sweated under the Loden cape, and noticed the hostility. 'Come back tomorrow to register', they said, 'we are closed'. But I had to register that day in order to stay the night in the country. In other words, bribe us if you want to be moving around legally in this country. I did, having no choice.

This accompolished, I went back to the train station. The local train to Pannonhalma turned out to be filled with farmers, hens and some old people. It was in fact a steam engine, the first and last I have ever ridden. Pannonhalma station was a stop in the middle of nowhere, where we got out on the railroad tracks – some hens and their owners, and I and my luggage.

The abbey was above the village, standing majestically on the hill. It had been the owner of the land of every family in the village for centuries. The road, winding up the hill, was a long and steep one. I could not walk up there with my luggage and Loden-clothes.

There was however a small house which must be the station building. I went in. Yes, this was a public place. I had been told that I could just take a taxi from the station. So I asked the only person there, who must be the station master, exactly that. Again the answer 'nincs' – 'does not exist'. He naturally spoke no German either. I pointed up the hill to the abbey. He offered me a cigarette and said a lot which I failed to grasp. We smoked together in silence – like a peace pipe among Indians, I thought. The type of cigarettes was the same, awfully strong communist brand that I knew so well; 'Sophiae', they were called. What a sight it must have been, like the theatre of the absurd: a lady in heavy Loden, obviously from Vienna, next to a little Hungarian station master, puffing away in silence on a quiet afternoon in the middle of absolutely nowhere. He also offered me the strong plum brandy that is drunk everywhere.

This reminded me of a film about a stationmaster's daughter, Klarika. The film is about the trains that never stop at her station, while she waits for them to do so, in the summer heat and slow life in the countryside. This is the entire 'sujet' of the film, because the train never stops.

Finally my friend called me out with him. He had an idea. Producing his scooter, he pointed to the back seat. I hesitated. Travel in style? I was beyond this point a long time ago. So I got on, but was too heavy with my luggage on the bumpy dirt road. We gave up, and I started to resign myself to a life like Klarika's at Pannonhalma station.

The solution came when the stationmaster finally got hold of the abbot by telephone. Hitherto such a simple idea was hindered by someone in the abbey who claimed that the abbot was away. But he was not, and I was collected by two young Benedictines in a van.

They could not understand why I had not taken the hourly bus from Gyor.

Notwithstanding the difficult journey, I had a tremendous welcome there. The abbot was a wonderful old man, nearly eighty. He was already a legend; people knew he stood up for them and for his principles. All those long years of communist harassment and isolation, all those delicate negotiations about the school and the abbey: How many new priests could they admit to the seminary? How many school boys? Which school books were allowed? He had, as stated, been maltreated by the police on a regular basis. But he was beyond fear; otherwise he would have succumbed to the pressures long ago.

It made a very great impression on me to meet a person like that and to realise that the values one stands for are more important than life itself. To give one's life is the ultimate demand Christ may make on you, but it is a relatively rare occurrence, and most of us are never asked for it. But to meet someone who had stood the test so eloquently, was so impressive.

It was the Easter vigil, and all the monks and the visitors went in procession into the dark church, candles in hand that were lit from the first light inside. It was timeless. There had been Easter vigils in this church for a thousand years. The contrast between the sterile and hostile communist officialdom and this Christian community was tremendous. Here, in the abbey, there were all the faithful from the villages around – poor farmers, but with such big hearts. To them, the Benedictines were much more natural than any Communist. They came to the Fathers in the abbey like their natural fathers, asking them advice on everything.

I met some relatives of the abbot, two elderly women, who 'adopted' me immediately. This generation of Hungarian women were so hard-working and so poor, but so hospitable and cultivated. Despite the language problems, they would continue talking with me, feeding me as if I were an orphan.

They later took me in their 'Trabi' – the omniscient East-German car – to the border crossing at Hegyeshalom, arguing angrily with the guards who tried to forbid our taking a farewell photograph there. 'Don't forget us', they said.

I never will.

In these people Christian virtues were second nature. They behaved radically differently from their Communist neighbours. How could this be? I was fascinated by this fact. I had never met such dignified people who were without societal support systems. True, they had belonged to the educated and cultivated class, but that was in the past. Now they had nothing. But they had their faith, strong and genuine. They were ready to live that faith in societies that really persecuted them. I, on the other hand, kept my faith in a private world and didn't care for my own society.

Gradually I started to reflect on this – on the need to go beyond the private sphere if one is a real Christian.

Complacency in the West

It is annoying that people talk about conversions as if they were made once and for all. In fact, when one is received into the Catholic Church one does not make any final step, albeit an important one. 'Conversio' means to go back, to turn back to God. It is a continous process that lasts as long as one lives. Nothing is ever certain on this way. All that has been gained, can be lost. One needs to renew one's will to conversion every day, and every day means beginning again and again – and again. Nothing is certain, nothing is won, until the end.

The usual talk about conversion is illusive; it connotes that people can make this step and then relax spiritually for the rest of their lives. This is false and deceptive. There are conversions every day; every day you get up after having fallen and renew the will to follow the difficult yet joyful path of Christ. No one is 'saved', as they used to say in my childhood town. Only God saves.

I converted, as one says, in 1982. I lived for many years after that in what I call a state of 'Sunday Christendom'. I went to Mass every Sunday, and lived the rest of the week as if that Sunday had no implications for my everyday life. I fulfilled the obligations of the Church, and thought myself a good Catholic. I was in fact quite satisfied with myself.

What does it meant to be a Christian? What's the point of going to Sunday Mass? One is strengthened by the sacraments. But for many years this was for me only a refuge when I was in need, a comfort and a joy. But it meant nothing really in terms of my life and my behaviour. It was like two worlds – my life was in one part, my faith in another. And the two never really intersected.

The Catholic Church in Norway is an immigrant Church, made up of more than one hundred nationalities, but consisting only of about 40,000 persons. The Norwegians make up the minority, of approximately 12,000. Many of us are, like me, converts from an academic background. There were some writers and intellectuals among the converts after the Catholic Church was legalised after the Reformation, as late as in 1864. These converts had usually met Catholicism abroad, through studies, especially in Italy and France. But the Catholics were no normal part of Norwegian life – to be a Catholic is in a way to remain a foreigner, to be something un-Norwegian. It speaks for itself that I was the second Catholic in Norwegian post-Reformation history to hold national political office, and the first to be a member of the Christian Democratic Party.

I mention this to underline this separation of integral life in Norwegian society and the Catholic faith. The Church, with its three bishops all being foreigners – even German in a country once occupied by Germany – kept a low profile in Norwegian life. Its priests rarely partook in public debate, and wished to be uncontroversial. But implicit in this is also that the Catholic Church to this day remains outside Norwegian society in a very basic way.

This is relevant because it sharpened the division I gradually felt more strongly in my own life. I was a Sunday Catholic. I led a double life. Nothing was really integrated of my faith and life. I lived by Catholic norms; but I kept my faith a private matter, and I was content with this – for a very long time.

Then came the crisis.

I started to become so frustrated by the passivity of the Church. Why weren't the priests active in the public debate? Why were they so much outside of society? In the face of all the controversial topics of the day, why didn't they react? Weren't they supposed to lead us? My husband, of a traditional Hungarian background where lay people had little role and the clergy and the Orders were the Church in a basic sense, did not understand my complaints. The Church should stay away from all this, he opined. I disagreed with him, but my own frustration was really a frustration with myself.

The problem was not so much with the clergy, but rather with the laity – in other words, with myself. I realised that my Sunday Christendom was superficial and that I did not really have much faith. When some personal problems became rather acute, this was accentuated. I was thinking the unthinkable: that I was ready to leave the Church.

In late 1992 the whole family stayed in the Benedictine Abbey of Pannonhalma in West Hungary.

In Pannonhalma I had found an invaluable friend. He was old and wise, yet young and open-minded. He was, like those who live a truly spiritual life, full of joy and youthfulness despite his advanced age. He represented the very best of the Benedictine tradition. As I had gained in insights from my Dominican friend earlier, I had now been blessed by a continuation with the very best of Benedictine spirituality. This monk was a fountain of living water.

The Benedictine connection

I owe a lot to the Benedictines. It all started when I was in Rome with my mother in 1981. I was not yet then a Catholic, but had a fascination with the Church. As mentioned, my husband went to the famous Benedictine gymnasium Pannonhalma in West Hungary. He stayed there for four years, and received the best humanistic education there is. One of the Benedictines from that abbey, Fr Gerardt Békes, OBS, was a professor in Rome, at Sant' Anselmo up on the Aventine Hill. The major abbey of the Order is quite modern, yet majestic. I knew the name of this monk from Hungarian friends, and decided to ring him.

'Do come anytime', he said, and told me the directions. I walked from the hotel where we stayed, my mother and I, all the way up on the Aventine Hill, traversing Rome from Via Cola di Rienzo, where our hotel was. The ascent to the Aventine is a beautiful little way that ends in the garden of the major Dominican house Santa Sabina, even more interesting than Sant' Anselmo because it is much older. From there one sees Rome and St Peter's.

I was asked to wait for the Benedictine in a pleasant room with a view to the inner garden. There were dark green trimmed hedges there. I was a bit nervous: What would I talk to him about? And why had I asked to see him? Monks were not supposed to be disturbed too much, and I was not even a Catholic at that time. I had heard that the Benedictines were awfully learned, so I resolved to talk about philosophy with him as this was at least a plausible subject for both of us.

I had expected someone very solemn, perhaps stern. But the man that came was quick, humorous, and made me feel at ease. He was certainly no introvert intellectual, and took a great interest in meeting someone as exotic as a Norwegian with Hungarian friends. The conversation was light, yet profound: I suddenly found myself talking about my interest in the Church, but not in a personal sense, more in an intellectual sense. Faith was something one could talk about in a perfectly rational and intellectual manner, I learnt. This man was at the same time a practical person with both feet solidly planted on the ground, but also fully at home in the whole European philosophical tradition.

He invited me to Mass on Sunday with my mother. She came reluctantly, but was taken with my new friend despite his being a monk.

I kept contact with him, and he was to become pivotal to my development as a Christian. I could always turn to him, and we had long conversations about things spiritual between Oslo and Rome. When he 'retired' at eighty – still being extremely active, he moved back to Pannonhalma after nearly sixty years in Rome. He continued to teach and travel, write and lecture, visiting us in Norway many times.

He was so young of heart that I often felt old. Once on a bus in Budapest he said. 'I am over seventy, so I don't need a ticket, but you are only around fifty, I guess, so you must get one.' I was furious: 'I am thirty-five! How can you think that I am fifty?' He was genuinely sorry, saying that he was not used to sizing up women! That was certainly the case. But I never thought about him as being an old man.

We were the best of friends, closer than most. He regarded me as his spiritual daughter, and was as enthusiastic as me about scholarship and the European spiritual tradition. With him in Pannonhalma there was even greater reason to go there.

But this time there, in December 1992, I was unhappy. I told him that everything was so difficult, I am such a hypocrite; I don't believe anymore and my faith has no implication for my life. He looked at me and simply said, 'You probably need an absolution'.

I was stunned. I had not been to confession for more than the required times, and had never really known what to make of this sacrament. 'I will come to see you this evening after the children are asleep', he continued.

I hoped that he would forget about it. I had a baby

whom I was still breast-feeding, and the whole family stayed in one of the hospital rooms of the monastery in order to have enough space. The other children were slow to fall asleep, and the baby was crying. She kept awake until almost ten o'clock, at which time I was sure that the monk had forgotten. I felt very relieved.

But he had not. He came. We walked in the corridor, a Baroque splendour. I was so utterly unhappy that I had none to turn to but Christ – the typical pattern of someone proud. I never thought the confession would 'work', and had wanted to avoid it. But my Benedictine friend had come, and here we were. Better to get it over with. It was at least good to talk about one's problems with someone who could give good advice.

So I talked, there in the dark corridor.

Then a most unexpected, stunning thing happened. A wave of intense joy swept over me, unlike anything that I had ever known. I cannot explain it in words, but it was a turning point in my life as a Christian. God – until now a rather distant entity – became a personal God there and then.

The flame of that experience lasted for a long, long time. Now I was longing for Christ, my friend. It was not a theological possibility, but a reality that was intimate and personal.

It was the second time Christ made Himself present to me in a direct manner. The first was in the Dominican garden in Oslo – the surprise that Christ is a person, alive. Also that time I had been not only surprised, but scared. Yet it had made a major difference – it made me make the formal conversion.

The second encounter was even more powerful. It was equally surprising. It is almost impossible to write about. But it was a major turning point.

Looking back many years later, I somehow think that stubborn people like me would never have gone further on this way without such 'jump-starts'.

I went back to Oslo with the family, and after some days I wrote my friend: 'I feel really stupid to write this to you, but there in Pannonhalma something awesome and joyful happened.'

As usual, he was a hard man to shock. 'Be grateful for such an extraordinary grace', he wrote back. 'Pray more.'

CHAPTER 4

REAL LIFE

When one looks back, after some years, one sees a certain logic to things. Above all one realises how little one knew, and how blindfolded one was. The ultimate horror in life must be to see nothing coherent when one looks back, only events that are unconnected and that lead nowhere. If life is a journey, as we often say, this implies that there is a route to be followed; a road to be travelled. That also means that there is a goal to be reached. But for very many people they think that there is no such goal, and hence no road to be traversed.

The goal for many is material wealth, which is the prime mover in most of society. To earn more, to buy more, and to be happier. It is enticing. I, too, want this or that. I have to watch myself. It is so easy, also for a family, to become centred on things as the goal, not as a means to a pleasant life.

The goal is not only money, but also power or status. The three go together: your income tells others how important you are, and your title reflects this as well. It is good to be ambitious, but the problem is the direction of the ambition. When I forget my real goal, and get caught up in the frenzy of seeking influence and money – and I often do – after a while I get this terrible feeling of emptiness and boredom. I obviously seek the wrong things; work for the wrong reason. Worst of all is the feeling that there is nothing there to strive for; it is all vanity for the moment. This feeling is also what creeps in when you amass new things. You enjoy buying, acquiring and buying more, but then, at some point, the same feeling of being far off the track. There is no satisfaction of a deeper kind to be had.

Retrospectively, one may see a certain development in one's life; one sees mistakes, one sees detours, and one sees progress. One sees how some things were preparations for later events, and how some skills were necessary for what came afterwards. One sees, in glimpses, perhaps – if one is really blessed – the finger of God. Lucky the person who has this experience!

The contrast between the senseless life and the struggling life is the difference between death and life.

But if life without direction is the normal life today for most people, how can there be anything else? This Christian claim to give meaning to life sounds like a naive fairy tale, like a sweetener in an otherwise tough world. It sounds like the fantasy for the weak, like Nietzsche said. Happiness? Tell me about it.

When I was young, I detested the Christianity I found in my home area. I thought the Christians there were unreal, escapists from the real world. Perhaps they were, at least many of them. But I was also stupid at that time, and unkind. I had not yet love for other people.

But what I came to discover over the years was that Christianity is realism – the only realism. Only when you are truly realistic, can you stop escaping from the world, and you find may real life in the middle of the world.

Realism means to see life as it really is, in all its grimness. Life is short and death is approaching every day. The death of the body can be gruesome. Illness, disfiguration, old age, mental and physical breakdown. There is nothing as dead as a corpse. The *person* you knew and loved is gone. He or she is not in this dead body anymore. Gone, often with total absurdity: an illness, an accident – like a flame of a candle blown out.

When I was a young girl, serving in the first aid unit of the Red Cross, we often searched for drowned people along the coast and at sea. Once we looked for a man for several days, using long ropes with hooks on. His grown children were with us in the boat, assisting. On the third day the rope caught something heavy. It was him. It was so strange to realise that this has been a living person just some days earlier, happily fishing as usual. Now he was like a stiff log, so inhuman. Death changes everything we know about human life.

How can we stand it? How can there be any meaning to such a horror?

Then there is the grimness of life lived without any happiness, any meaning, any joy. Those who never break out of their own confining circles, who go to a job they detest year in, year out, who live in 'hopeless' marriages, who break up and are lonesome, who are 'failures' in the eyes of all others. All the ambitions of youth, never attained, all the misery of life, and the injustice. When death comes, such lives seem to have left no traces behind. What was the point?

There are millions and millions of such people – who never manage to make much of life and who perhaps never have the chance. Poverty, lack of education, all sorts of reasons. Can they have meaning in life? Can they have happiness?

Christianity is full of paradoxes. Blessed are the poor, blessed are the meek. What kind of happiness is this? What's the point of a poor life where the person never has any influence on anyone? Can such a life be one of perfection and bliss?

Yes, claims Christianity. It is much easier to find God if you are meek and poor, because you then tend to be more humble. You have to forget yourself to find God and to be happy, and you have to die to yourself in order to live. What does this mean?

We have all read it, and probably rejected it as nonsensical. How can I forget myself, even less die to myself, when all that I have is this 'myself'. Today we are all so self-centred anyway. It would seem impossible to forget oneself, even for a single moment of spontaneity, which does occur. But most of the time we are centred on ourselves and our own will.

After Pannonhalma

On my way back from Pannonhalma after that divine 'kick' in December 1992, I saw things in a new light. It had been a complete surprise, this experience of a flame of love; and I was somewhat numbed by it. What did it mean? I did not know God, but He knew me and my needs. I remember that we participated in some EU conference in Copenhagen on the way back, that while on the aeroplane I read about the separation of the Princess of Wales, but that all was like a review of things passing by.

Back in Oslo, it was dark December and Christmas preparations. I did all the usual things involved in this hectic work, but had an inner 'flame' that was burning, a joy of an encounter that I could not describe. It was like falling in love secretly, and guarding this secret for oneself.

I talked a lot with my Benedictine friend. He urged me to pray and listen. My new insight after this was that I must do something in my field of knowledge and interest, viz. my professional field of politics. Somehow Christianity must also be in the middle of this world. I had no idea how, but now at least I saw that I must do something myself and not wait for the bishops or other official church representatives to act for me. I had been so frustrated over the fact that the Norwegian Catholic Church was isolated and passive in our society. Well, what about my own responsibility?

The practical manifestations of this took the form of re-establishing the local commission on Justice and Peace in the diocese. I found out that there was this kind of commission also in the Vatican. Looking through the annuario of the Vatican in the bishop's office, I came across the name of a monsignor in the pontifical commission. I called the nunciature in Copenhagen, eagerly asking them to make an appointment with him for me. The person on the other end of the line said: 'Who are you and what do you want?'

But after that initial cold shower I became a close friend of the nuncio and his staff. I went to Rome to see my monsignor, and we talked for more than two hours. It was a meeting of like-minded souls, and I was extremely happy to have met someone that was fully engaged in the issues I loved.

I also eagerly delved into writing some articles for a magazine run by Jesuits in Brussels. To my complete surprise one of the articles was rejected. It was about the right to life and the lack of implementation of this right – about the contentious issue of abortion in Europe. The article was rejected, I later learnt, because it stated the church position directly and without any 'palliatives'. The editors feared that it would be seen as controversial by some readers. I was stunned. I had thought, in all my innocent love for the Church, that her representatives would be clear and strong on matters of faith, and the issue of right to life was such an issue. I learnt, however, that there are many conflicts within the Church, some of them ugly and nasty. But I was still naive, and tremendously disappointed at this discovery.

That flame that was lit in Pannonhalma was not extinguished, although I did not pray much at all. I was still looking, not knowing for what, but knowing that there was something to be found. My meaning was in this field in some way: Christianity and politics.

I had been frustrated over the lack of ethics in political science when I was a student, wanting to recover the classical tradition of *summum bonum*. Now, many years later, I learnt that this is what the Church was trying to do, in the middle of the world. Like a piece in a puzzle; this learning many years back was suddenly relevant and useful. But how? What was I to do? As yet I had no idea.

Copenhagen

Decisive steps in one's life are seen as such only much later. One such step came in February 1995. I was at home with flu. It was late morning. I sat at the kitchen table revising the manuscript for a book which was based on my doctoral thesis; it bored me immensely. I have never been patient or conscientious. I want results quickly, and am easily bored. The book was on the energy policy of the European Union, a topic I had chosen because I happened to know a lot about energy and because I wanted to write about the EU. So when the telephone rang it was a most welcome interrruption.

It was the monsignor I had met in Rome from the Council for Justice and Peace. He asked me to be a member of the delegation of the Holy See to the UN's Social Summit in Copenhagen in the beginning of March. I was intensely happy and honoured. I knew that this was important in my life, but not why or how.

I was happy because I was going to represent the Holy Father; serve him and work for him. Non-Catholics cannot understand the point of this. But for a Catholic, the Church and its spiritual leader, the Pope, are much more than the empirical reality of the organisation. It is the Church of Christ; a community of the faithful which is much more real than the physical structures. One gradually grows to love the Church and the Pope – the Church despite all the deficiencies in her members, and the Pope ever much more because he carries such an inhuman burden in being the Vicar of Christ on earth.

I loved Pope John Paul II and I always prayed for him. He was mild and kind; quite different from the media picture of him. When I saw him so infirm and tired in his last years, I loved him even more. He was another brother in Christ, like the rest of us – his main title which he preferred to use was *servo servorum Dei* – literally the servant of the servants of God. But the Pope is also the leader of the Church, with the burden of leading her for as long as he lives. He alone must bear the responsibility, and he alone must make certain decisions. He is entrusted with much more than most of us. His must be a very lonely life.

I had never imagined that Rome would ask me to do anything. Oslo seemed so far, far away. I was extremely joyful, and couldn't wait to tell my husband when he came home in the afternoon. This was after the infamous Cairo conference on population and development, in September 1994, where the Holy See had been blamed for much of the confrontation. The Norwegian prime minister at the time, Gro Harlem Brundtland, had launched very harsh and unjust criticism, and there had been quite a prolonged attack on Catholic views on abortion and family planning in the press here afterwards. It was not pleasant to be a Catholic – on the contrary. So I was a bit apprehensive about how my fellow Norwegians would react to one of theirs representing the Holy See.

The time of the conference came, and I had not received much by way of preparatory documents. I was upset about this: why didn't they prepare more? I wondered what I would be doing there. It seemed a bit disorganised, or perhaps I was a bit too Germanic.

On a Sunday afternoon I travelled to Copenhagen and was met by the nuncio, who took me to the hotel where the delegation stayed.

There was a delegation meeting that evening. I was happy to meet the ones I did not know, and the monsignor who had asked me to come. His name was Diarmuid Martin, currently the archbishop of Dublin. He was always so joyful and funny to be with, as well as intellectually one of the sharpest minds I know. Irish, he had a wit second to none. But most of all I was impressed by his political sense, which was combined with profound intellectual insight. I was the only Scandinavian there.

Later, when I have worked in other Holy See delegations, I have derived a tremendous intellectual stimulus from interacting with these diplomats, who are educated at the world's oldest and most prestigeous diplomatic academy. I have never been as much appreciated for my brains as in the Vatican, as well as for my motherhood.

The Church was the institution in Europe that started universities and also the one which started education of girls and women, and there is a long tradition for intellectual women. Woman are mostly respected for their intellect in most places in the West today, but it is rare to experience this unconditional acceptance of both being a mother, being feminine; and being intellectual. 'Stay in touch, I need your brains', my good friend Thomas Cardinal Winning of Scotland used to tell me. That pretty much sums it up.

The work these days in Copenhagen was intense, largely because we were such a small delegation. It was my first international conference, and I learnt a lot. I enjoyed it immensely, for it is one thing to study politics from the outside, quite another to actually participate in it. The Holy See was this time uncontroversial, and contributed greatly to the success of the summit.

On the first day I decided to walk across to the Norwegian delegation to introduce myself. There had been a little article about my participation in the press at home. The Norwegian diplomats looked at me. 'Are you with *them*?', a blond lady asked with some disdain in her voice. I affirmed that this was true. There was no enthusiasm on their side, to say the least.

One of the delegation members caught my attention. He worked very intensely, and seemingly very well, but seemed not to get stressed like the rest of us. He was serene and very helpful to all of us, including the least important. I think this feature was the most remarkable about him – that he was equally nice to everyone. He was a layman like me.

One day I came across him reading something from Scripture as he sat by his computer. We started to talk. I was intrigued by him: How could be work like that, in such a pleasant, detached way? Why didn't he get stressed or irritated, like we did? He was just one of us, yet there was something different about him, especially about the way he worked. Naturally I could not ask him directly about this, but I knew somehow that this man had a secret.

And I wanted to find out what it was.

There was an occasion – a dinner à trois. The third person was another laywoman. I remember we talked about how lay people also have a vocation, and that this vocation is as important as that of clergy – it is just different, not less. From all the conversation that evening – which was to turn out to be revolutionary in my own Christian life – I recall his saying: 'Unless you find God in the middle of the world, in your work, in your everyday life, you'll never find Him. You serve Him when you wash the children's clothes just as much as when you speak at the UN. It all depends on the how you work, and on being united to God all the time.'

The next day I had to leave because the children were left all alone with my husband, and I had a job to look after. I hurried to the airport, leaving all my new friends behind. I knew that the meeting with the other layman had changed my life, but I did not know how. I only knew that the key word was 'vocation'.

A vocation for lay people?

After my return to Oslo, life went ahead in its usual way. But I was preoccupied with the things this other layman had said, and more than that, shown in his manner of being. There was something there, but I did not know what. He seemed to have a lot of joy in his life; in fact, he was happy all the time. I was at that time so centred on myself that I could not understand at all how anyone could be otherwise. But I, too, wanted to be happy.

And I wondered: what was he so happy about? Was his job that interesting? Superficially, yes, but not in real depth. He must be tired of working in the media, with the constant pressures. Was his private life that much fun? He did not even have children, which most of us find to be the only real source of joy in our lives. Where did his joy come from?

I wanted to shake it out of him. Why didn't he seem to feel restless, and bored? How could he have this mastery of himself; and more than that, have a constant joy? I envied him. I had to find out how this happiness was possible. It could not come from the outside, but if it came from the inside, how could I discover this secret?

What was this talk about a specific lay vocation? Did that make him so happy? It didn't in the least seem like the fulfilment of my life. Did it really fulfil his? It must be some sort of put-on. Could his work really give meaning to his life? I, too, loved my work, but I had never thought about it in such terms as a vocation. I sought fulfilment from it: needed its challenges, loved to work hard, to achieve, to write well, and so on. But to make it a platform of service to Christ? My work was only fulfilling when I really became absorbed with it because it was interesting. But I could not see that it was really connected with Christ in any way. Yet this layman claimed that his work was; and that this was the raw material of his vocation; that in fact it could become a service to Christ; and thus his 'conversation' with Him. I understood that such a prospect could bring happiness, but not that it was a possibility. My work was just my own work, and nothing else. If I did a good job of something it was satisfactory, in fact a tremendous satisfaction just at that moment. But then the boredom and restlessness set in afterwards; when there was not such a brilliant and exciting result.

I did not fathom how he could make this boring work of his – and boring it must be a lot of the time – into something else. The 'thing' I wanted to grab was this secret source of joy that had to be there in order for him to tick – unless he were a master actor.

With my usual impatience I would have liked to attack him: 'How can you be so happy all the time? Aren't you bored out of your mind there? What do you do?' I wanted that joy, too. Now. Right away. I wanted to get rid of my vacillation between joy in the Mass, serenity, some enlightenment, peace of mind – and the hurly-burly of work life, of everyday life, an ordinary life which was light years from that peace. I had understood that Christianity must be incarnated in the world, but had no idea how. I was still looking for God for myself, and perhaps having some idea that I should bring Him to others, but it was not at all clear how this could be possible.

My Hungarian Benedictine friend of eighty-two was also of this happy constitution. Whenever I phoned him in his monastery in Pannonhalma we would have a long and joyful conversation. Also he lived for something else, in fact for someone else – for Christ. I was still far from this, but was vacillating between serious attempts at so-called abandonment, and complete self-centredness. That was going to last for a long time, but I had no idea of this at the time. One can only understand these things afterwards, with hindsight.

I thought that my Benedictine friend had a special 'professional' Christian standing with God. He was a contemplative monk – although an extremely active man – and he was also a professor of ecclesiology. He must know God much better than I did, and after all, he was the one who had a vocation; a special calling from God to be a monk. I was 'just' a layman, one of the large majority of Christians, but not an 'expert'.

My Benedictine was by no means this clerical type that you sometimes meet. He had a very lay outlook, and we were sparring partners in philosophy, meeting as often as we could. He started all sorts of projects – lectures, seminars, meetings with young people – all over Hungary, where he had returned upon so-called retirement at the age of eighty. For him that was no excuse for resting: when he got back to Pannonhalma he organised vast initiatives and seemed to travel all the time. So he knew and appreciated my lay world, but he was not part of it.

Becoming it, not reading about it

At this time I started to discover that the accent was on becoming Christian in my actions and deeds, in fact in my very being; not on reading about it, like an external 'thing'. My Benedictine friend used to advise me: 'Try to forget yourself', he would say. I was frustrated. I who was preoccupied with my spiritual abandonment ...! How could I forget myself? At this time I had been reading enough spiritual books to fill a library, and had tried to find out how far I was in my abandonment, which was the goal of all mystics. There was one particular book by a Swedish Carmelite, Wilfried Stinissen, called *Fader, jag overlamnar mig til dig* ('Father, I abandon myself to you'). I bought it in Stockholm in 1995, and it became my favourite reading and *vade mecum*.

It was divided in three parts; the steps on the way to abandonment. The first was entitled 'accepting the will of God', the second was 'doing the will of God', and the third was named 'being in God' or something similar, describing the contemplative state.

I used this book in the wrong way; reading it like a 'how-to-do-it' manual. I was interested in how far I had come towards the desired state of abandonment, and I tried to use my will to get there. So my self-centredness continued: had I reached the first stage? The second stage, perhaps? And were there possibly any signs of the third stage? I analysed the 'diagnosis' of these stages over and over again, looking for 'symptoms', and the book eventually became leafy and torn from over-use. It is an excellent book, but I used it in the wrong way.

This whole exercise was naturally quite ridiculous, because it led to the very opposite of abandonment, which *presupposes* a forgetfulness of self, not an intense concentration on the will to achieve a goal. But my will, strong and stubborn, held on to its grip. I still had not understood much about what love is.

From Copenhagen onwards, however, I knew that there existed such a real possibility of incarnating Christ in everything and in every activity in the middle of the world, and I desperately wanted to know how to do it, because my own happiness hinged on it. At least I knew someone who tried to do it.

There is a Norwegian expression which says that one 'limps on both feet', which means that not only does one limp, but on both feet at the same time. That is of course impossible if you need to walk. But that was nonetheless how I felt. Put differently, I rode two horses that moved in opposite directions. One steered towards the serene, private Catholic life of Mass and prayer; the other was at home only in the world of activity, work, business, and politics. It was schizophrenic and could not continue. I felt the discrepancy between my 'private' Catholic life and my work life more and more acutely. I did not want to go to Rome or somewhere 'Catholic' any more, like my Benedictine monastery in Hungary, for then to return to Oslo and lose my peace of mind immediately. I had to be fully Catholic here, every-where, in every situation. Often I realised how deviant my behaviour was from what it could have been; when I stopped to realise that my being a Christian was not detectable by anyone. There was nothing about my way of being that indi-cated the presence of Christ; and this I could see much better now than before. In those places that were 'Catholic' I would become inspired, full of resolve to change, so that I would effect change at home. But once back in my home country, so decidedly secular, all was like before. I did not even want to be there. I actually wanted to flee from the place where God had put me.

But in the midst of all this I had had a glimpse of a unity of life in someone else who even claimed that this was a specific lay vocation. For me it was like coming across a life buoy on the sea.

The Thirst for Joy

I think the only real motive for the religious search is the search for happiness. It is a natural thing to want to be happy. Chesterton was once asked why he was Catholic, and replied: 'because I want to be happy'. This is not a selfish desire, but the deep need for the human being.

True joy is connected with love, and love is only

possible when you desire the best for the other. This sounds like nonsense as long as your will and your self hold on tight to your own steering wheel. So much that passes for love is really devoid of joy: the possessiveness of someone who wants the other on his own terms, like a prize. There can be and is tremendous desire in such love, often to the point of self-destructiveness, but it is not joyful love. It is possessive love, owning the object, not respecting the other or setting him or her free.

But joy comes suddenly to us when we let the ego off guard for a moment. For instance, when someone needs help, and we give it, without calculations. We just do something good without expecting a reward. It is almost surprising that we do it, used as we are to calculating the returns. The Pharisees always had these *arrière-pensées*. Therefore they had no joy.

Joy is like a breeze; it disappears when you try to catch it and tie it down. But we have all known it in rare moments, when we did not expect it. It is a tremendous experience to do good because then one is completely human. Then one also becomes shameful, another rare experience for many people.

I sat with my eldest son, waiting for the street car. An old, brittle lady moved slowly across the street, obviously on hard times. She looked in the waste baskets to find empty bottles to earn a few kroner. I felt so ashamed that she should have to do that. We helped her across the street, and I offered her some money. She was very thankful, far more thankful than she should have been. I had really done nothing, and was shameful because I thought to myself that I had done something good that day. Just like the Pharisees. But however mediocre my service had been, there was a little joy there, because there was an act of love, however small.

The strange thing is that where there is joy, there is love. One becomes happy when one does something for love of others. One should think that it is the other way: one should become happy when one acquires that which one desires: isn't that love? But the breeze cannot be caught and put in a bottle; it moves freely. Joy is only present when one does something for others, because at that moment one forgets oneself and is free of oneself. The attraction of my layman friend was precisely this joy. By comparison I was full of worries, which is a sign of self-centredness.

The experience of self-forgetfulness in brief moments is shared by all human beings. It is undeniable that there is a joy resulting from being of spontaneous service to others. One feels a freedom that is unlike any other experience; one of happiness because the self is not longer the frame of reference, but something or someone outside this self. Clearly the self is like a straitjacket much of the time.

In the Gospels there is the story of John and James, brothers, and disciples of Christ. They had served and followed Him for a long time. They had understood that it would not lead to earthly kingship or power, but they nonetheless tried to get a concession: We will serve you, they said, even until death – but then we want to sit at your side by the heavenly throne and reign with you. That was the reward they wanted.

The habit of calculating returns lies deep in us. That is why the selfless service makes such an indelible impression. How is it possible? When we meet people that seem to act selflessly, we can hardly believe it. What makes them do it? Isn't there some ulterior motive of gain? Yet we know from our own experience that it is both possible to serve or do good without calculation, and that these moments give us a tremendous joy.

As an expert in international politics I am used to thinking with sinister motivations. One famous story that illustrates this inclination in politicians and analysts is the anecdote about Count Metternich, the famous Austrian diplomat. While in the midst of negotiations with the Russian ambassador, the latter died. The Count was troubled: 'I wonder what he intended by that', he reportedly said.

The Christian message is truly paradoxical. Serve the least among you, said Jesus, and did it. You must die to yourself in order to live. He who seeks to save his life, will lose it. The grain must die before it can give rise to life. Humility is a precondition for 'seeing' God and knowing Him. All this speaks of the need to be like a child in front of a Father: helpless, needing, dependent.

Yet all that we are, seems to be different: Self-control, control of the environment, possession of things and people. The cramp of the grip of the self. The only thing we cannot control is death.

These two extremes of human life are mutually exclusive. Most of the time we live with the self as centre, but we also catch glimpses of another reality which is within reach and which promises a joy we can taste when we finally abandon ourselves by forgetting ourselves.

There are stories of people we know who give up money and status to serve. They go to impossible places and live on very little, but are happy. They claim that the service gives meaning to life. I read about a Norwegian teacher, a single woman, with a good income and safe life, who sold her house and went to live in the slums of Rio, to work for the street children. She does not want to return to Norway. She has found meaning in her life.

Others do similar things, like devoting their lives to helping the poor in Rumania, gathering clothing, driving trucks up and down from northern Norway. When I visited our troops in the SFOR brigade in Bosnia, they briefed me on all their military tasks and demonstrated the weapons. But at the end they showed me, with enormous pride and joy, their little 'invention': a 'lifeline' of supplies and daily contact with the local mental hospital in Modrica. Each week supplies were sent by the Norwegian army on trucks from Oslo to Bosnia. The spare capacity in the trucks was filled with donations from various organisations, and the tough military men took this to the mental hospital where they were loved and embraced the way only mentally retarded persons can. Did they have to do this? Not at all. The mental patients in places like the Balkans are worth nothing in these societies – they are isolated and neglected like the worst outcasts. In Kosovo's only mental hospital, which I visited right after the war, the Serbs had simply passed by, massacring the neighbouring villages, but not cared to enter the hospital.

The Norwegian troops had no 'rational' reason – like supporting civil-military relations – for their engagement at the mental hospital, but they did it nonetheless, and it gave them this noble joy of helping the most needy. It was moving to see how the dirty, malformed human beings there excitedly greeted their friends in green.

Thus, there seems to be this hidden and reluctant urge in us to serve others, although we do not give in to it very often. The interest in the self is mostly overwhelming. But some people are better at service than others. They need not be Christian, but they often are. And even if one does not believe that Christ is the Son of God, incarnated and risen, one must necessarily be struck by the words He speaks on the subject of service. The demands are tremendous, yet there is promise that we can do it.

In my bookish attempts at abandonment I had been reading all about the stages of self-forgetfulness. It seemed like a recipe to be followed and then, like magic, it would happen. But I had not understood that it cannot be deduced, it must be done. And it can only be done when one struggles, in practice, to imitate Christ. I needed to forget all the words and the books, and to start DOING.

Christianity is also eminently material: one does not live one life of the soul, and one of the body. There is no dualism, although many have thought so in placing so much stress on the life of the mind. But Christ is either in the middle of where I work and live, in my everyday life; or not at all – or at least, I would never find Him. The incarnation must mean a real integration of Christ in everything created, not on the side of it. Clearly this is not the case in much of the world, but that does not mean that it is impossible.

This way of seeing the world surprised me because I had thought of my Christian life as a life between God and myself, extending to the private life of my family and friends perhaps, but not one of a radical new look at the world: infuse it with Christ, it depends on you.

I recalled that my friend from Copenhagen had told me that his vocation was in his work in the place he lived, although he also had said that he missed his home country and his former profession. OK, so he was no superman: he had loves and likings that his vocation did not permit, and he had to struggle to stay the course. That was at least something. He was a bit like me. It was not as easy as it sounded for him either. It was not a once-and-for-all match that you win: from now on I am serene, happy, and in a state of abandonment, ready to serve others and to forget myself.

But nonetheless he was very certain about his vocation: that he had one, as a layman, and that it consisted in making Christ present to others, in every human activity. But how was this to be done? The logic of it was of course convincing, but the practice? There were some moments where I could recognise the peace of Christ in family life and even in political life, but most of the time it was as if that peace was to be found in the Mass only, and that the moment one left the church, the world and all its demands descended upon you and disturbed that peace.

The Joy that comes from Love

I came back to the question of joy again and again. C.S. Lewis called his story of becoming Christian *Surprised by Joy*, a strange title, it seems. But the quest for joy is deep and real, and all men have it, even if they don't know. We seek happiness in things, in human love where we may find it, in experiences, in hopes and dreams. We are on the outlook for something called joy. We catch glimpses of this joy from time to time when we are spontaneous, helping someone, doing a service. With children there is always joy because they are in need of us, not having utilitarian motives, loving us as we are. There is a lot of joy to be found in life if we are open to it.

I remember being at a gathering at the offices of a Christian newspaper in Norway where I have a column, occasioned by the bestowal of an annual award on someone who has served fellow men. This year the prize went to the Salvation Army and its so-called 'slum sisters', women who give out food and other aid in the poorest areas of the city. In Oslo in the year 2000 there were also many people who asked for such help.

This sister was one of the solid women from the fiords of western Norway, used to tough weather and a tough life in general. She spoke this typical Western dialect; strong, direct, matter-of-fact. She emanated strength and practical common sense. She related how her daily work was, and spoke about the Salvation Army, not about herself. At the end of her speech, she paused, and said: 'So why do we do this work? Because the love of Christ forces us.'

Her frank manner made for few flowery phrases. It was all down-to-earth, like this: The love of Christ forces us. That was her experience: she loved Christ and knew the joy of His love, and then she felt she had no choice: He expected her to bring that joy to others. I am sure Mother Teresa and a few others could say the same.

Perhaps the joy of Christ is the necessary spur to make us do all the work that we otherwise would never do. The slum sister in Oslo would never have done this grim and sad work without her being in love with Christ.

I had become a Christian because I sought truth, and found it intellectually, via deduction. But once I started to frequent Mass, I was drawn to the source of joy in the sacrament. I always came back, longing for this joy that could be found there in a completely mysterious way. I fell in love with Christ, not knowing how or why, but finding myself in love. That is something absolutely different from deciding that the evidence pointed to the truth of the claims of Christianity.

Then the long period of 'riding two horses' started: all the years of 'Sunday Christendom' and the dissatisfaction with this way of life. There must be more, or there is nothing, I had concluded, and had almost left the Church.

But I was helped back, like a child who loses the way and cries out for help. The experience that God was personal, and that He knew me, is awesome and tremendous. After Pannonhalma I knew that He could act on me; that He had helped me. So I had started to bring more unity into my life, realising that it was possible to be fully Christian – somehow. It was like being blindfolded, having to rely on someone else instead of on myself. Hitherto I had relied on my will and my plans, now there was the choice to rely on Him or continue the old way.

I started to realise how little I knew Him and actually believed in Him. When you read the Gospels, you see that His contemporaries had exactly the same problem. Wasn't He just the carpenter's son from Nazareth? Even when they witnessed the miracles, they did not believe, and we would probably be equally unbelieving today. The only certainty I had was in fact the knowledge that this unspeakable joy and peace existed. I knew that it was real, and it came from Him. It came as a surprise, always – in the middle of the street, perhaps while I was working, when I did not think of Him, but also when I had made an effort to find Him. I knew what C.S. Lewis meant by the title of his book. I was just as surprised by joy as he had been.

'God is love', one says so easily that it sounds like a cliché. But this is what God really is, and that is a deep insight. Once we have tasted that love, that joy, nothing else satisfies us. In his moving *Confessions*, St Augustine writes, 'Too late did I love you. You were within me, but I did not know it.' This knowledge came after many years of futile life, and came as a surprise. I don't know why also I came to experience this – we call it grace, a gift – but one thing I know with total certainty: this joy is unparalleled. It is without doubt the deepest and most real joy that a human being can experience.

The mystics have of course written about this for centuries. It is Christ's personal gift to all those who honestly seek Him, and He speaks about it in many places in the Gospels – about the peace He grants, which is not of this world. We see it very clearly in St Paul, whose heart is filled with joy and love during the worst of tribulations. So we should know that it exists; yet it is impossible to explain to those who have never known it.

But this was what kept me seeking – the remembrance of that joy and peace. It is perhaps easiest to define it negatively: when one is 'off the track', one feels empty. When one is 'atuned' to God, one knows that one is on the right way somehow. For those who are used to living in the presence of God, there is not this vacillation and thirst for feeling. It is a sign of the beginner in the spiritual life: one is not yet so experienced that one knows that God makes His presence felt in glimpses, and that the joy of knowing this presence is a gift, but not something to race after. It should not be the motive for what we do, yet it is often the motive for the Christian who is not yet very 'advanced' in his or her relationship with Christ.

It could be compared, I think, to falling in love versus being married. The person who has just fallen in love is only preoccupied with the sight and presence of the beloved; yet it is in a way a selfish search: for personal and exclusive joy. The married person who manages to stay married is usually no longer in love, but loves in a mature and self-giving way: the relationship is one of structure, predictability and concentration on the work that the spouses do, e.g. with the upbringing of children. Yet this does not mean that there is less love, but that the love is not centred on the personal and selfish experience, but is a love for the good of others.

Meeting Christ is to fall in love, or not to meet Him at all. It depends on one's willingness to meet Him of course, but also on His grace. It is a mystery that so many never seem to care about Him although they have heard about Him. I do not understand why it is so hard to discover Him, but many people have a hard heart. They are not interested in Him as he is, but only as they would like Him to be. He comes to those who earnestly seek Him, even though they may not know that it is Him that they seek.

But he cannot be had on my – or on your – terms; only on His own.

Christ for my needs?

But what about the world? Finding Christ for me was essential, but it was only the necessary condition for becoming Christian. The Christian life does not consist of the two of us, but of all of us. That was my major challenge: to bring Him to others. So much so-called Christian life is safe and sound within the ghetto: the ghettoes of the Catholic Church, of tradition, of our Lutheran Churches in the North – in short, a life lived on the side of real life in the world. What a contrast to the apostles and first missionaries who, like crazy zealots, set out into the wilderness of the pagan world without any help at all. I count myself fortunate to live in one of the most secularised parts of the world: at least then I know that whatever little faith I have, it is real; not the product of favourable circumstances.

But the problem was still the world. I had rejected the escapism of all those who live on the sidelines, happy with their cosy little Christian lives. That was doomed; it was not meant to be that way. Either Christ was to be in the middle of the world, or the Christian claims were partial, false, not real after all. I knew from my Benedictine friend that his monastic vocation was real enough, but also that it was not mine. I also knew that this talk about a lay vocation must be true for my new friend from Copenhagen; the 'evidence' I could see pointed to that. But how was it possible?

Everything in the world can be filled with Christ, as it was intended.

This is easy in theory, hard in practice. Our lay vocation is also contemplative, as we need to be contemplative to remain Christian, especially in the middle of the world, but this vocation is different from the monastic ideal. It is to make the world Christian from the inside.

Knowing pagan life as it is commonly lived today, this is a very hard task. Therefore the lay person needs perhaps even more of a contemplative soul, because the distractions and temptations seem overwhelming. How can anyone live chastely when sex is everywhere, in every shape and form? How can anyone be detached from money when materialism is the name of the game? How can anyone love by giving oneself for others when egoism is the natural and acceptable point of departure?

I had always found intellectual solutions to the issues. That is how my way to the Church has started. On the way I had been helped from the intellectual recognition to an existential experience of God's personal relationship with me; and a flame had been lit. I had gradually realised that I was not going to be a type of appendix to the Benedictines or the Dominicans, and that my place was somehow in society and politics. In Copenhagen I had met another layman who claimed a lay vocation, and that was a key issue – how to bridge the 'private' Catholic life and my daily life.

Only in retrospect does one see what was true and what was false. I went back and forth between trying to live a full Christian life in my work, and between just pretending. There were long periods of dissatisfied boredom where I felt that I could never, ever be a witness to Christ. Then He made His presence felt again; and I was full of joy for a short while. But since I relied on this feeling of presence, I 'gave up' when it disappeared again.

If only I had known the importance of a steady inner life at this time, much less time would have been wasted. But I did not. I had little spiritual stamina, and felt sorry for myself. I wrote articles about what it meant to be a Christian, but I did not yet know that it requires a lifestyle that fosters and nourishes an inner life of closeness to Christ. I ran into my own difficulties over and over again, wanting what I could not have; rejecting what I already had and the cross therein. In short, I did not trust in God the least; only in myself. I wanted human happiness; not any suffering. The result was a lack of taking the bull by the horns, and a continued distance to the implementation of any practical spiritual programme that would make me face some tough realisations.

How could one find God in the middle of the world, when one did not find Him inside? I had found Him; or rather, He had let me find Him, but despite all these graces of His presence I depleted my spiritual resources immediately when His presence was gone because I made no real effort to renew them. I made all sorts of excuses to myself: no time, no need, I will do it later when I feel like it.

My Benedictine friend put it this way: 'Sometimes the clouds disappear and you see the sun. Sometimes He seems to "forget" you for two months, even a year; but He is there all the time.' I agreed in theory, but had no will to 'train' for my inner life with Christ when I did not see the relevance of it. With hindsight I know that these periods were of major importance, but I neglected them. So I had no resistance or perseverance when the going got rough.

Heaven and hell are inside; this much the great saints have all known. They knew their defects, and fought them with determination. The paradox is that the more 'refined' your conscience gets; the more you see your defects. But until you are at this stage, you don't know that you need the help that spiritual direction and the sacraments offer. Your ego is so big that you have no need for God or for any help.

Again, with hindsight, God is the supreme pedagogue. I would never have 'needed' Him unless I were in a situation where I could not see the way out. I was trying to find my human happiness, and thought I had found it; thinking that God could be added to this picture. He would do my will, as it were. Then I realised that there was His will for me, something entirely different; but I was in no hurry to explore it. I was not actively seeking His will, but was only open to it when I could not realise my own will.

The times when I was on God's 'wavelength', somehow my love for Christ entered into the work and contact with others. I also felt a deep happiness when this was the case: to bring Him to others was the only worthwhile thing to do for me. But those moments were sporadic.

I had read so much about abandonment and self-forget-fulness. Those were only words to me. How much nicer it would be to live with mastery of self, without longings, impatience, without this feeling of loneliness that the modern individual has. I had now been a Catholic for more than fifteen years, and seemed to regress rather than progress. What would God want to use me for in Norway? It was a hopeless place anyway. Why couldn't I achieve the peace of mind that I wanted? Why did I commit the same stupid errors over and over again?

I indeed longed for that abandonment.

I had come 'full circle' in the end: I realised that without an interior life of faith and prayer there could be no apos-tolate in the world. I saw the 'divine logic' in the lay vocation for me – this was my field, where my profession and faith met – but only much later did I really understand the importance of being close to Christ. I learnt the need for this through reluctantly getting to know my own cross, and defects, in short, getting to know myself. I had to climb up that slowly inclined plane of gaining an interior life in order to be useful as a Christian in the world; but also in order to be happy, to become what I was meant to be. It was not going to be easy, as things so far had proceeded by failings and smaller and greater crises, but it was the only way.

CHAPTER 5

INTERLUDE: IS GOD IN THIS PLACE?

Rjukan

The name 'Rjukan' is dialect from Telemark, the mountainous country that extends to the large mountain plateaux between Oslo and Bergen. It means 'smoky', and refers to the smoke that falling water produces: When large masses of water fall hundreds of metres down, in other words a 'waterfall', there is smoke – in reality small droplets of water. It looks like a mighty cloud that underlines the powers of nature: the rumbling, frightening sound of the tons of water hitting the mountain, sounds that make one think of an awesome nature-machine at work.

Such a waterfall is in the deep valley which is now named 'Rjukan'. The Rjukan waterfall was one of the mightiest and wildest in all of Norway – and there are many – and was the natural place to build an electrical power plant and industry that was energy-intensive. This was thought out around the turn of the twentieth century, when Norway's mighty waterfalls started to become 'tamed' by industralisation. Eventually Rjukan went from being an extremely remote and gloomy valley to becoming a major industrial community.

This valley, Vestfjorddalen, was thought to be uninhabitable. It is a narrow fiord 'arm', so narrow and with such high sides that the sun does not reach down in the valley until April, and leaves for good in the autumn. The industrialists had to build a lift that would bring the population up on the mountain plateau in the winter season in order to make anyone want to live in such a place.

I sit on the train and think about this as we pass Hjuksebø, a little station up in the mountains between Oslo and the south. This is where we got off the train when I was a little girl, coming from my home in the south. We were going to visit my grandparents in Rjukan. They had come there from other places in order to find work, and also because my great-grandfather, a sailor skipper of a large schooner, suffered from asthma in his old age. He was advised to move from the coast up to the mountains – not an easy move.

Rjukan was for me the place of childhood joy in winter. I did not realise how harsh life there really was, or that it was an extraordinary place, even by Norwegian standards.

We got off at Hjuksebø, my parents and I and the dog, in dark, cold winter weather. It was always very snowy, and it was always extremely cold, right before Christmas. The stationmaster helped us up to the ferry. This ferry traversed the Tinnsjø, a fiord with extremely uninviting landscapes: dark, deep, among steep mountain sides that did not allow for habitation. I remember standing in the front, looking down at how the ship cut the ice. The large bits of ice were brutally forced aside as the ship moved through the only ice-free passage in the fiord.

The ferry was named 'Storegut' – 'big boy' in the local dialect. It sounded beautiful to me. This was the last leg of the trip to see my grandparents, a trip that was only possible in this way, for the snow effectively closed the road across the mountains.

As a child, I always thought that the temperatures of minus twenty–thirty were normal in winter. In Rjukan this was in fact so. This area is the home of skiing as we know it – the first cross-country skiier, and the alpinists reputedly came from there, and of course the 'Telemark-skiing' in loose snow, suddenly today resurrected and made famous again.

When I came onshore from the ferry, the sound of the snow was there when I walked: crisp, crisp, like chewing on something. It is great fun to make these sounds with one's boots. We have all sorts of names for these sounds that do not exist in English. Mild weather was what people there hated most: it meant rain and slippery roads. Mild weather made people, including us, really depressed. Snow and cold weather was the right thing: the breath was white fog, and the hair was full of ice, cheeks red like apples. I loved it.

My cousin, a boy five years younger, was waiting for me. We built snow men, bathed in the snow, got frozen so that we could no longer feel our feet. My grandparents lived on the mountainside, and the car tyres needed steel cables in order to drive up the road. When we came for the annual Christmas vacation, I was the happiest child on earth. I remember driving up the hill to their house: would we make it? Or would the car stop? It all depended on the ice.

In that home none was Christian; in fact, they were hostile to Christianity. Some relatives who were Pentecostals always tried to talk to them about the faith in ways that would make any sane person angry. My mother once went with them to a prayer meeting where they talked in tongues. Afterwards she hated what she knew of Christianity.

The quarrels with these relatives destroyed every propect of religion in the home. In fact, it provoked the very opposite effect. Even on her deathbed my grand-mother refused to see any priest, getting very upset and angry.

My grandparents were Socialists. That did not go well with Christianity. Rjukan was an industrial place, one of the foremost in Norway, and those who had come there from the coast, where they were sailors, fishermen, or farmers, became industrial workers. That meant not only socialism, but communism. My great-uncle Arve, whom I remember was the nicest and funniest man I know, was in fact a Communist. He represented the Communist Party in local politics, and a had a naive and touching belief in the Soviet Union's societal model. When he learned of the purges, of the invasion of Hungary in 1956 and of the repression and power politics of communism, he was really heartbroken. He, like so many Norwegian Communists, left the party. He never wanted to talk about this afterwards. His grief and bitterness was total.

These were times when Christianity was a bourgeois affair for a certain social class, and when the only Christians of working-class stock came from coastal Norway. To my father and his family, socialism and even more so, communism, were incomprehensible and frightening phenomena of a new time. In the family there were many late-night discussions which I could hear through the bedroom wall. My mother was naturally also a Socialist, and the topic was often about 'how much damage religion had done in the world'. These discussions were like normal evening rituals, a dialogue of the deaf between two worlds: my father's traditional coastal world where society was pre-political and apolitical, Lutheran in a very genuine and integrated sense; and my mother's world, where class differences were evident in everything in a constructed industrial society where heavy industry was everything.

But God was certainly present in my grandparents' house. They were Christ-like, I would venture to say, even without knowing it. They were full of love, not only for me, but for others in the community, and had an honesty and virtue of work that was enviable. My grandfather worked in the famous Vemork factory, erected on the waterfall in order to use the electrical power generated there. During the Second World War this factory produced heavy water (D_2O), a critical component in producing the atomic bomb. The German occupiers wanted to speed up this production and ship it to Germany, while the allies kept saboteurs – my mother's friends – ready up on the mountain plateau, for action to stop this. There were bombing raids almost every night, when my grandfather worked the night shift. The allies tried to stop production, and throughout the war Rjukan was a strategically important place. Finally the ferry loaded with heavy water was blown up by my mother's friends. Long after the war, when I was a little girl, I remember Kirk Douglas and the American film team which came to make a movie about this, *The Heroes of Telemark*.

My grandfather's night shifts during the war had their consequences. There were periods afterwards when he could not work. My grandmother was a rock – strong, resilient, in charge of everything. She was a practical woman, the 'man of the house'. I have never seen anyone who worked so much. When she got really tired, in the evening, she was easily angry, but never with the children. Her husband depended on her, and so did the rest of the family.

When my mother was a girl, during the war, my grandmother sewed clothes from old uniforms. She designed really smart things, for both her daughters, and made all kinds of outfits. She was famous for her ability. The food was hard to get in those days, so they all went up in the mountains to hunt and gather berries – nature provided both meat and fruits. Again, grandmother harvested and made jams and all kinds of dishes from these gifts of the wild. It was a necessity, and she was a master at using all these resources. We took it all for granted: the meals, the new clothes, that she could fix everything. She really loved us with deeds.

She had a large kitchen, its window facing the snow-filled, steep mountainside. The kitchen was the best place of all. Outside the window she had a bird-house, where the few birds that do not migrate in winter had their abode. I sat on the inside watching them. At breakfast she asked: 'What do you want for dinner today?' We were eager to go out skiing, and could not care less. 'Make something easy', my mother would say, but to make something 'easy' for twelve people – all of us visiting – was ridiculous.

Then we took off for the day's adventure; she always remained at home. No, she did not want to join us: she wanted to prepare our dinner, and supper, and so on. To come home from a day in really cold weather, to strip off the wet clothing, take a hot shower, put the ski boots in front of the fire to dry, and then – to sit down, hungry like a bear, to a dinner well prepared – that was love with deeds.

She always did it, we never noticed it. Of course she would have wanted to go with us, at least sometimes.

I was too young to appreciate all this then. I just relished the naturalness of being there and being taken care of by the grandparents. I recall the entrance hall of the house; how one stepped inside full of snow, freezing after hours of play outside, wet everywhere; and how all the snow from the boots was left inside on the floor. The hall was cold, like in all old houses, so the snow did not melt right away. That hall was somewhere between inside and outside, and a pleasant smell of old wood and winter. My grandmother took all these clothes – layers upon layers – putting them in front of the stove to dry. Mothers in the north appreciate summer when one knows all the work with children's clothing in winter.

In the bedrooms it was always freezing cold, a habit from Britain I think – the traditional Norwegian always sleeps with a window open, and has thick covers filled with down to keep the body warm. No one would heat a bedroom, and going into one from my grandmother's kitchen was extremely unpleasant.

The 'religion issue' was a dead one in our family, and my grandparents never met anyone who could show them that Christianity is not about gloomy people who talk about doomesday and speak in tongues. My grandmother was especially angry at these Christians. They also belonged to my poor grandfather's side of the family. 'They will leave this house if they talk about the "religion issue" ever again!', she would tell him. They, on their side, thought that they had a mission to accomplish with the 'pagans', and continued to make quotations about hell for those who did not believe. The fear that this instilled destroyed a lot for my grandmother, who died after many years of illness. Each time I tried to talk with her about God, especially at the end, she reacted with anger and rejection.

I have been deeply sceptical of all attempts at missionary activity since my childhood, no doubt shaped by these and similar experiences. It has to be done by example, and in no other way unless the example is there first. I have met so many imposing, disrespectful 'missionaries' in my time that I know what I am talking about. Being well-meaning is no excuse. There are many Pharisees around, as in Christ's day.

Oslo

One evening at dinner in 1997 at the German embassy in Oslo there was a phone call for me. It was the new foreign minister of the coalition government, led by the Norwegian Christian Democratic Party. I did not know him, had hardly heard about him. 'Will you become my vice-minister – state secretary in the Foreign Office?' he asked. 'If you start tomorrow at seven a.m., as I am off to China for two weeks with the King.' I was stunned. 'Why me? I am not even a party member; there are no Catholics in the Christian Democratic Party at all.' 'You have to join the party', he said, 'but they are very happy if you will, as the first Catholic.'

I acccepted; and joined the party, somewhat sceptical about the all-Lutheran political party, but convinced that being vice-minister of foreign affairs was made for me, who had studied and analysed international politics for many years.

This political service brought me to many places, and almost continuous travel, for the next three years; I had plenty of chances to look for God in strange and dangerous places.

But what was most interesting from a Christian perspec-

tive was my new party affiliation: the Lutherans there
were very good Christians, but their only political 'ideology' was the Ten Commandments – not bad as a basis, but
not as a way to communicate politics in modern, secularised life. From the moment I joined the party, however,
I knew that I was completely at home there: they were
believers, courageous, my fellows. And I could provide
them with a natural law-based ideology which was also
Christian – all that was to be found in Catholic social
teaching. Within a short time I was appointed leader of the
party's ideology committee, and wrote up the document
that forms the basis for its new ideology, built on the
pillars of the family as the basic cell of society, subsidiarity, and solidarity – the very principles of Catholic social
teaching.

'Finding' and working in this party was a piece in my
life's puzzle: I somehow knew that it was meant to be.
These rare moments which usually come suddenly in life
also contain a clarity that is striking: I knew that this was
good; that this was worthwhile. The way one knows is
through the inner peace and happiness that one is given;
through a deep knowledge that this is right.

But mostly one does not have this kind of certainty.
After the government was ousted in March 2000 and I
returned to the university, I did not at all see what was
meant by that. I felt restless and dissatisfied, and had to
accept to be patient, waiting to see what the next piece in
the puzzle would be.

God seems to act in this way: sometimes it is very clear
where He leads; sometimes there is no indication. The
latter periods are probably tests and training; in trusting
Him, in perseverance and patience.

My unexpected role as a Christian-Democratic politician brought something new – natural law thinking – to
my party. The three years of public office also taught me
that God is where you least expect Him: in people who are
far from Christ in nominal terms; in places that are in war
zones or in poverty; and among those of non-Catholic
creeds as well. Labels are not important; charity is. Also

those who do not know our faith and our sacraments are often filled with God's love as He is free to impart His grace. In those years of foreign service I was particularly impressed by the altruism that moved many workers in NGOs in developing countries and in war-torn societies: once they had tasted the joy of self-giving, they came back to these places, leaving the safety of Norway.

The Balkans

In my work as as state secretary I was most of all fascinated with the Balkans. These states are in the balance between good and evil and it is visible everywhere. Human evil has no limits; and in the Balkans, in our Europe, this is also demonstrated today.

What attracts me is not this, but the struggle to overcome evil. Is it possible to make normal civil life out of civil war situations? What makes the human being lose all barriers to evil, and what makes him regain those barriers? And how can we, with our money and other help, make a real difference? The only way is to create stable economic and political conditions, change the incentive structure and get rid of the political entrepreneurs of nationalism. But on a deeper level, it is to restore a sense of human dignity, which is the only basis for mutual respect among people and ultimately, for politics itself.

I am not surprised by evil and the propensity for evil. It is not far from the public stigmatisation of a group and the sanction of violence against it to the engagement of ordinary men and women in this violence. But most of the real terror in Bosnia and Kosovo was carried out by paramilitaries, trained for the purpose. When I discussed this matter with a French general of the Foreign Legion who had served in every trouble spot in Africa and the Middle East, he said that when you have killed once, it is easy, and you do it again and again unless stopped. The only decisive step is the first one. After that the barrier is gone.

I think he was right. In Bosnia it was the Serbs who

started the killing, but after a while all three ethnic groups were involved. The planned massacres were carried out by military and paramilitary units, but apart from this, the killing was done by old friends and neighbours. Once it started, the barriers were gone. Another logic was at work.

To kill is not in itself so hard to understand: in self-defence or war, it can be necessary. But the killing of the innocent is much worse to comprehend, and this is the sort of killing that is typical in modern armed conflict. Ninety per cent of all casualities are civilians, but civilians are also the protagonists. In the Balkans in the nineties we have seen killing, torture, mass murder, rape, all kinds of cruelties done to civilians, often by other civilians. Does this mean that God lost all His power in this place? I can easily understand that one kills, but not that one does it deliberately with the intention of torturing the innocent, even children. In the Balkans we saw this again and again. How can God allow it? Is He completely absent there?

Vukovar in 1998

Before I became responsible for Norwegian Balkan policy I thought that the expression 'after the war' meant the Second World War. But it doesn't. It refers to the gruesome war in Bosnia and Croatia from 1991 to 1995.

We drive down from Budapest on our way to Zagreb. I am escorted by Norwegian special troops who work in Bosnia. They don't say much, but are the more efficient. They are always looking around, watchfully. Then they make sure that we never step on grass. Mines. This is rule no. 1 in the Balkans. Never step on grass or dirt roads, always only on asphalt. When I got home from these trips I automatically avoided the grass for the first few days.

Vukovar was destroyed by the Serbs in their offensive in 1991 which started the whole war. The brutal attack and siege lasted for a long time. The water tower above the town is the symbol of the city. When it fell, the Serbs bombed even the local hospital, and afterwards killed all the patients who were hiding in the cellar. The destruction is still enormous. The whole city centre is in ruins, and the task for the international community is to rebuild houses, schools, and to get investments for jobs. The unemployment rate is still about ninety per cent.

It was a beautiful town in the Habsburg monarchy, a pride of Croatia. Now it is totally destroyed. The Catholic church is bombed to pieces and stands like an empty shell, peppered by bullet holes.

What can we do there? The intensity of the hatred for each others' religion is blatant. The first places destroyed where always the churches or mosques. As late as in 2001 – six years after the war – the international representatives who came to lay the foundation-stone for the rebuilding of the famous mosque in Banja Luka were attacked with stones and fire by the local Serbs. They were trapped inside for seven hours; some wounded. That mosque had been on the UNESCO World Heritage List.

I met all the local rulers in the region of East-Slavonia: Vukovar, Ossiek, some smaller towns. We have a lot of asylum seekers, Serbs, who are discriminated against after the Croats regained the region in 1995. Now the Serbs will be returned from Norway, as they do not fill the critieria for political asylum. Yet I understand that anyone from this poor place would want to emigrate, and make up any type of reason for it.

Norway gives a lot of money and aid in kind, compared to most other states. We kept Sarajevo alive during the war with our trailers of food that came over the mountains. The drivers constantly risked their lives. It was a major operation. Now we are fully engaged in Bosnia, Croatia, Albania and Kosovo. But the money does not bring miracles.

In the small towns of Serb population I met the mayor and the local dignitaries. They had pictures of Serb generals on the wall. They thanked me for the aid, but naturally wanted more. But rehabilitation of schools and houses do not help if there is no work. And who wants to invest there?

I left the misery in East-Slavonia to tell the rulers in

Zagreb that they must stop discriminating against the Serbs. It is always the same show: I say that we were worried about harassment of Serbs, they say that it may occur locally, but beyond their control; and anyway, what could one expect so soon after the war? The Croats are tough to the bone, and sophisticated. The Serbs are only tough.

In the local places of mixed ethnicity, such as in East Slavonia, they all know who is who: who is Serb, who participated in action, who did what. The revenge comes and the international community can do little about it. A murder that is never solved; the same pattern which is repeated almost every day in Kosovo.

The hatred is right below the surface. It is clearly there in my Croat counterparts, despite their polished appearance. The war is only a few years ago. Why should they forgive? Why should anyone turn the other cheek and forgive? This maxim of Christianity seems absurd in such a place. 'They killed my parents', says one. 'They drove out my family and burnt our house', says another. And when Operation Flash and Storm, the Croat offensive with American support, finally drove out all the Serbs from Knin and Kraijina, they also looted, burnt and killed. Revenge seems the only logical and honourable reply. Can a man forgive those who killed his family? Why should he do that? Christian ethics seem fine in theory, but who can say that it should be followed here?

'Don't ask us to forgive', the Croat politicians in Zagreb answer. They are Catholic like me, but their kind have been massacred. I am disappointed, but understand them.

There are 250,000 Serbs from Croatia waiting to return. They live in dire, awful conditions in Milosevic's Serbia. Will they ever come home?

But at the end of my period in political office I come to Zagreb for the inauguration of a democratically elected president – and the year after, in 2000, Serbia also experiences a democratic revolution. As professional politicians and analysts we do not understand how. It is a new beginning.

But the question remains: How can one forgive in such situations? I think to myself that it is only possible when one imitates Christ: He forgave and even loved His torturers. On a purely human logic, the response must be 'an eye for an eye'.

Bosnia

I continued to Modrica in Republika Srpska to meet our military personnel in the Nordpol brigade, which consisted of Polish and Nordic battalions, hence the fitting name.

Their camp was well protected, near the cities of Modrica and Derventa where considerable massacres took place. There were still many unopened mass graves. I had turned down applications for money to identify the dead several times. They need forensic equipment. The families were still waiting for their dead, whom they knew were in this or that mass grave.

How could I say no to such a request? Because the money was needed for the living. Housing was more important than identifying bodies. In Bosnia there are still thousands and thousands of dead who await identification and burial. In Kosovo we estimated about 11,000 murdered. Most of them are still in mass graves. The Hague tribunal needs evidence, and the UN excavation teams look for that only when they open graves. The difficult and long-term work of identification must be done by others. It cannot be high on the priority list: But can you imagine what it does to human dignity to know that your loved ones rest in a mass grave, perhaps never to be identified? A mass grave that is close to where you live?

The mayor of Modrica was a hard liner. The brigade had to be tough and firm. But they also showed me something beyond confiscated weapons and mines. They had 'adopted' the orphanage and hospital in town. They carried supplies – gifts from NGOs and suchlike – on the military convoys that went from Norway once a week. When there was room, they filled it up with things that were needed in these places. The patients and the children knew the green berets. In military jargon it is called 'cimic' – civil-military work – that is aimed at consolidating relations with the native population.

On one occasion I came with the Norwegian officers to an elementary school in a village in Srpska. We practised strict conditionality in granting money to local communities: if the mayor accepted minority returns, in this case of Bosnians and Croats to this Serb republic, we would give money for school buildings and material. This visit was to the first such school where the local authorities now hosted returns from Sarajevo of Croat refugees. It was still dangerous for them to return, which is why they were under our military protection. This was as late as in 1999, four years after they fled from their homes.

We entered a classroom with first graders. They saw all the uniforms, and ran into a corner of the classroom, screaming out of fear. The teacher went after them, comforting, talking in a loud voice.

'What's going on?' I asked, taken by complete surprise. 'They did not know that you are not dangerous. They are used to military uniforms on paramilitaries – those that came to kill them.'

After a little while the children were at ease with us, playing and joking, but it was eminently clear to me what they had been through and which traumas they had suffered.

Perhaps the future began for them that day; when they could live in their old village in safety. But the evil they knew, as completely innocent children, is impossible to accept. Why do the innocent suffer? We also know it from Scripture – how the baby boys were killed by Herod.

But we do not understand it.

Kosovo

On one of my trips to Kosovo recently after the bombing had stopped, I visited the only mental hospital in the province, in a little town called Stimhle. We had given money to the Norwegian Red Cross to run it and to hire nurses and psychiatrists. Since I was the lady with the money, they wanted to show me something nice. Thus, they took out the best patients in the yard.

But I could hear the noise from behind barred windows upstairs. They were covered with childrens' clothes hanging to dry. But there were small faces peeking out, curious at the visitor.

'I would like to visit the childrens' ward', I demanded. They tried to say no three times, but finally I just started to walk upstairs.

It smelt like a zoo – terrible, degrading, inhuman. Inside the rooms there was no light, but after a while I could see the children in their beds, some strapped to them. They screamed aloud, reaching out their hands to touch me. One little boy took out a cigarette from my purse, and puffed away happily. In the Balkans, children unfortunately smoke when they are little.

Another boy grabbed me and pulled me towards him. I thought he wanted a cigarette, too. But he put my arms carefully around him, one by one. Then I understood: he wanted me to hold him, to hug him, to be loved. From me he wanted the most basic thing in the world for any child and any human being: he wanted to be loved. He held me like that for a long time, smiling. Destroyed teeth, shaved head, mentally retarded or simply impaired by having been kept inside, strapped to a bed – a little boy like mine, a son of God, who loves him as much as any other creature of His.

I shall never forget that experience. In this ante-chamber of death; smelling of excrement and dirt, with no light and no hope, a little boy desperately searches for a little love from a stranger. So please remember that you can do a lot for children – your own and others – and that the love you give is worth much more than anything else..

There, in that hospital ward, in that little boy, Christ was present and I became fully human for a moment.

Then we drove on to a village known to all the world, Rajack. It was up on a hill. It was here, in January 1999, that the OSCE mission's leader, William Walker, showed the world press how forty-seven villagers had been massacred.

The Serbs had burned down the school and all the houses in the village. The schoolchildren met us in the yard, where they both played and were taught. It was still warm, so they could be outside. These were happy, joyful children, surrounding us foreign guests. We had given support for food and woollen plaids to the families living there, as they all lived in burnt-out shells.

Visiting one mother of a large family, I wondered how they could manage. Inside there was nothing but sooted brick walls, the smell of fire still pronounced. The mother said: 'It is hardest for the teenager. She misses everything.'

Later we heard that the small children went to play on the parent's graves. 'They don't understand that that they will not come back.'

How could God be with these people? One should rather ask: How can we be naive about the human propensity for evil?

Cuba

We went to Cuba, wanting to start a so-called human rights dialogue. Only Canada had done this before us, and the Cubans cancelled the whole thing with the Canadians when foreign minister Axworthy criticised them. Norway was in a better position, we felt: the Norwegian social democrats had ties with Cuban Communists, and we, the Christian Democrats 'inherited' this past. I had excellent contacts in the Holy See; and the Pope had just been to Cuba. The person who had 'engineered' the sucessful papal visit helped us to set up the key contacts. When the Pope was there, he was able to 'open up' Cuba to the world, at least for a little while. Two thousand journalists had followed him on the trip, and Cuban television was forced to transmit all the papal Masses. Political prisoners had been released, and the Pope had rightly criticised the US embargo, so Castro had some support as well.

The papal team had laid much important ground work. I could also use this as a platform for us. The Cuban politicians, my counterparts, trusted the Pope's press spokesman, who also helped me.

We went on an official visit in September 1998. Flying out of Madrid on an old Iberia 747, we soon discovered that the inside of the machine was rather worn and old. Then we noticed that the crew spoke Icelandic. The turbulence was already bad. So I asked my Latin-America advisor Herbert Linder from the Norwegian MFA what this was about. He had flown the route before. A seasoned traveller of less civilised spots in the world, Herbert said dryly: 'I just checked the cockpit. The pilots have their feet up, relaxing. The crew is hired by an Icelandic cargo company which operates this flight. That is either good news, or very bad news.'

Nothing more was said. This was yet another occasion to have a drink and leave it all in somebody else's hands. As my husband used to say, flying in strange planes is a good way to become more religious. I had flown in all sorts of tin boxes in the Balkans, so this was just another such experience. But it is true that these are great occasions for realising how one depends on God.

In Cuba we were welcomed, and conducted a press seminar with Norwegian and Cuban journalists. The first evening we had a bacalao (bacalao=cod) reception, a major success as Norway had been exporting stockfish to Cuba for many years before Communism. Our counterparts all had reminiscences of this delicacy.

My meetings included the cardinal, the nuncio and other church representatives. Their analysis of the situation for Christianity in Cuba reminded me of my communist experiences from Hungary: a cat-and-mouse game with the authorities, based on intimidation and threats from the latter, but also granting some concessions. My political counterparts were of course aware of these meetings, and both church and political authorities amicably joined each other at our reception. But the repression was real, and here there was the Cuban equivalent of

Kremlinology: any changes in the *nomenklatura*; any new moves from Fidel?

He and the US government both needed the embargo, like masochists who both need the punishment and actually enjoy it. Without it, Fidel's power would vanish, and Cuba would have to live in real time. Now it is like a museum, and people visit it for just that reason. But still old-fashioned repression continues, with imprisonment of oppostion and no freedom of religion.

The nuncio impressed me very much. He was very serene, detached, and pious. In the nunciature where we talked, he turned on the classical music. There were microphones in the walls, but they were too pretty to tear down. So we spoke to the music of Mozart.

The human rights dialogue got started, with the agreement that all sorts of mutual criticism was allowed. The Cubans wanted to speak of social and economic human rights, while we spoke about political and civil rights. Of course they used us: it was useful to tell the UN community that they were engaged in such a dialogue. It was one way of avoiding criticism. But beneath the utility function of this kind of consideration friendship grew through our meetings. Friendship is first of all based on respect, and I have discovered that much of international relations consist of just such relations – of people in key positions in various countries who know each other and help each other find common solutions.

The Cubans were no different. They had of course been taught that their communist system was the superior one to our capitalist one, and had the island mentality of apprehension, suspicion, and a certain inferiority complex because their system evidently showed no progress in the world. But I discovered that they were very proud, sensitive to any lack of respect. They sensed that we treated them as equals, and that we respected them. They clearly appreciated that, and could even, in private, talk about the problems and shortcomings of their own situation. Naturally they were furious about the embargo and the United States, with every good reason, I must add. They were also insulated from the influences of normal interaction because of their own system. But they were very hospitable and warm – light years from the Communists in the Soviet system. They were Caribbean and Hispanic; full of laughter and temperament.

My Cuban counterparts became even better friends when we could discuss the topic of fish. The fisheries minister was happy when he realised that I had read the young Marx and we could talk about alienation under capitalism. In most bilateral foreign meetings ideology never enters into the conversation. But we had a full evening of conversation about fish and fish farming, and about the young Marx; by the beautiful seaside where Fidel and Che had come onshore that onerous day when the revolution started. The fisheries minister had known Che, and was proud of it. The next day he sent me his articles about Che and Marx, with a nice inscription. We decided to try to collaborate on fish farming. The bacalao was too expensive to import.

The last thing I knew about that, was that our Norwegian exporters sat drinking *mojitos* with the Cuban colleagues in the afternoon breeeze on the terrace of Hotel Nacional, so perhaps ...

Is God in Cuba? In many many travels and meetings in the strangest places I always looked for that something that would bring the joy again. It was not to be found in systems or things, but in people. When a conversation would turn to the real subject of the meaning of life and of how to find it, I would become really engaged. These moments came unplanned and were about laying the basis for friendships. A sympathy for the other, an offer of openness and help, a willingness to trust the other and to share knowledge about the human experience. Such relations would always be based on mutual respect.

In Cuba I made several such beginnings, because they understood that we were equals, respecting them. At the end of the talking, when the politics changes and wanes, these relations may persist and grow. And they may even contradict political orthodoxy and make lasting impressions. Politics is often a ritual, and both sides know it. They play their roles accordingly. But the human factor, when it 'intervenes' can be stronger than any role play.

I left Cuba with my newly acquired book of Che photos, bought at twelve US dollars in Hotel Nacional, at far higher than the market price. I decided that this was a new variant of the system which should be called 'commando capitalism'.

Almaty

It was one of those sudden trips that I had started to get used to in my job in the ministry. Norway was chairman of the Organisation for Security and Cooperation in Europe (OSCE) that year, and my superior, the foreign minister Knut Vollebæk and I had to go to all the trouble spots in the Balkans and in the former Soviet Union on the spur of the moment, if the need arose.

This time he had to cancel his trip because of the Kosovo crisis, and I was his substitute. The destination was Almaty in Kazhakstan, known in the Soviet period as Alma-Ata. This city is familiar to Norwegian ice skaters because of the competitions held there, and the training which was sought after due to the high altitude of the location. It is virtually next to the Himalayas, and from the city one looks directly up at the snow-clad mountain massif which forms the border with China.

The trip was pleasant, given the length: seven hours' plane ride, but in a modern Lufthansa jet. Upon arrival I was met by our embassy personnel. It was in the middle of the night. Despite my diplomatic passport there were forms to be filled in, and many check points in true Soviet style. The road into town was bumpy old asphalt, and the hotel must once have been a pride of communist architecture. As usual in such places, there were lots and lots of employees who seemingly did nothing and who spoke no English. The senior lady, who spoke Russian, insisted on showing me a suite of rooms. She obviously thought I wanted something big. I insisted that I was just an ordinary person wanting a single room. But to no avail – I had to see the suite, a terribly depressing living room in dark brown with mammoth furniture and an enormous bed, no doubt the pride of the hotel. In private I have a little competition for the ugliest hotel in the world. There are many candidates. So far Hotel Bosna in Baja Luka – the most authentic combination of Balkan ambiance and communist architecture I have seen, is on top of my list, but this one was a possible competitior.

After a lot of resistance the *babuskha* gave up: I was not giving in to her offer of a suite at only DEM 390 per night. I finally got a room at half the price, and could go to bed for another short night's sleep.

The next morning I looked out of the window to see the magnificent mountain massif above. There is something frightening as well as majestic about mountains. No human can master them – they touch the sky in their silence. I once passed, by plane, the highest peak of the Andes. It is a terrifying, awesome sight to realise how little the human being is in this perspective.

From home I have learnt to respect and love the mountains and the sea. But in Almaty the *only* attraction was these mountains. People there were poor and the city was worn. It was the typical Soviet-type city – high rises of a monotonous kind; in bad shape, grey, unbecoming – placed in the middle of nowhere, on the Asian steppes. The Kazhaks are nomads, but were naturally collectivised like the rest of Soviet citizens. Now they are poor, longing for western investments, on the verge of starvation in many cases. This is a developing country, like the rest of the Central Asian republics, but so far western aid has not been very visible. They need infrastructure, modernisation, democracy, jobs.

In the OSCE conference I was chairing, the local elite naturally came, including the press. This was a way of bringing some attention to the place, of teaching a bit about modern state craft and government, and of getting international actors interested. The locals were all trying to say the right things, and they were fast learners, like all people in need. The press was servile, trained in the Soviet period. In my press conference they did not know which questions to ask, so I lectured them on the need for democracy and rule of law, adding my criticism of the president's monopoly on power and on corruption. I don't know if they wrote any of that. In my Balkan experience I had learnt that it is necessary to say a few things very clearly, with as much criticism as possible of the local leadership. Then sometimes it would be printed and possibly have an impact. The best was always if I had a stick as well as a carrot: unless this changes, no more aid money. As bluntly as possible.

After my meetings with political leaders, voicing the same blunt criticism, I gave a reception. Standing at the entrance with my delegation, I wondered why no one came. A representative of the OSCE office in town finally came and told me: 'They are standing outside in a long line, more than 300 people, but they are waiting for you to signal that they can come in. They are used to being told what to do by the authorities.'

When they entered, they hurried to the buffet table. This was a rare occasion for eating as much as one wanted. It is unusual for us to think about people being on the verge of starvation, or at least living on a very slim diet. This is the case in Kasazhstan as it is in most of the former Soviet republics. At the reception one of the few foreign representatives told us that they now had a butcher in town. That was apparently a big event. 'Why is that so important', I inquired. 'Because until now they just sliced up the dead animal like you slice a loaf of bread', said the expatriate.

It was a great event, this reception. There was plenty of food, and I could see how they had all dressed up, with what they had. It touched my heart. This little thing, for me, but for some it was something spectacular. I went around with my interpreter to talk. They were so hopeful and nice, these young people – shy of the foreigners, hungry for development and opportunity, as are all young people. I thought to myself: How much good capitalism could do here! If only investors would not be so afraid of taking political risk. Jobs are what they need, but we also know that corruption is rampant.

Three young women from Europe were also there. I had been in contact with them before I left, as they were Christians who planned to work and live in Almaty in order to spread the gospel. They were modern ordinary lay people; who would make Christ known by implanting themselves in the middle of everyday life there.

I was amazed at their courage. They looked like they belonged in a safe, bourgeois European city. Instead they were here, in the poor, faraway place in the middle of the Asian steppe, where Christianity was unknown after decades of communism and atheism. If they had any religion to speak of here, it was Islam. How would these girls get jobs here, where unemployment was so high and corruption pervaded public life? One of them studied Russian to have some basis. They lived in very poor conditions, and were completely out of place, I thought. My motherly instinct took over: I was certainly going to tell those who sent them that they were irresponsible, and have them called back.

My European friends wanted to take me to the only church in town. We drove for a long time, through the most derelict and poor areas. It was singularly depressing: nothing but makeshift houses, poor people, dirt roads, and Soviet-style architecture. And so far from home, from Europe. I was depressed on behalf of the European girls. Their cause was hopeless. I saw that they had no money, no jobs, did not know the language, yet that they were so brave and determined to do this. They should go home to normal life, I thought to myself.

Finally we reached the church, run by the Franciscans. It was a nice, new building, a pleasant sight in an otherwise extremely depressed area of poor shacks instead of houses. The rain did not make it any better. Inside the church there were a few people for Mass, looking as poor as the surroundings. But the Mass could have been anywhere: it brought back the universality of it all. Outside, the awful reality of poverty and depression. Inside, the hope that only God can provide. It is good to be in these contrasting surroundings, I thought to myself, because there is nothing else to rely on. Either God is here – now, present – or He is nowhere, just an illusion.

Like so many times when I have been sad, without hope, irritated, I again experienced the reassuring peace of the Mass; as if He whispered, 'take courage, I am here for you'. One comes to Mass without faith, or with very little; but if one 'opens one's ear' just a little, there is help there. I have experienced this many, many times: everything is hopeless, I am restless and bored and without any joy. I go to Mass even if I don't want to. But if I only allow God to act, by being still there, He somehow restores me. God, how can I have so little faith after so many years? And how can you give me so much grace despite this?

The church was like an oasis in the desert.

I left Almaty and my new friends. They managed to be optimistic all the time, whereas I was the pessimist on their behalf. I took off the next morning at four a.m., being guided through a chaos of people and officials in the early morning. I was glad to be privileged: no controls, VIP; thinking, I am happy that I am not like them – the ordinary people. What a disgusting attitude! But I did not reflect on that at all – one gets used to privileges very, very easily. All the others had to pass through dozens of check points with uniformed guards, who were employed to do nothing but boss people around. This was third world, Soviet-style.

I shuddered when I saw uniformed guards by the plane, smoking. One cigarette too close to the plane, and a cata-strophy. Well inside I sank into my business class seat, watching the others struggle to get in. God knows how long they had been in the lines at the airport, probably having to give a bribe or two to get on.

I pitied my Christian friends who were left in this place, and wrote an indignant letter to their organisation when I got home. It is really irresponsible to send young people to that place, I said. Don't rely on your human reasoning alone, they very politely told me.

About a year later I was in Rome to address a student congress. After my talk a group of young girls came to the podium. They were from Almaty: my three friends, and some local students who came to Europe for the first time in their lives. The Europeans had found jobs, and were already attracting locals people to this Christian congress. They looked happy, and had all that they needed materially.

I was ashamed of myself: I had so little faith. What could explain these developments? Certainly not my all-too human reasoning.

Yerevan

I was in Spain with my family for the fall vacation. We sat in a university conference when my mobile rang. It was the foreign minister. Could I represent Norway at the state funeral in Yerevan the next day? The other ministers were all away, and I was the only one relevant left to ask.

I hesitated. It was a family vacation. My husband was good about it, seeing that it was important that someone from foreign affairs would handle it. And it was the last few days of the vacation anyway. 'Go', my husband said.

In Yerevan, we had seen on our hotel TV that there had been a shoot-out, as the Americans call it. Not just any shoot-out, mind you. No, this was half the cabinet of Armenia, and the president only survived because he was at the airport with the US deputy secretary of state. But his prime minister and six other ministers were executed by two killers who entered parliament and systematically shot them, one by one, in the head.

Yerevan and the rest of the Caucausus is a hot spot. The war in Azerbaijan over Nagorno-Karabakh had gone on for years, making Armenia even more isolated as the only Christian enclave in the region. There was talk about Russian involvement in the killings, since they did not want progress on the peace process, some said. Others spoke about an Azeri plot to destabilise and weaken Armenia, while the official version was that the killers acted on their own, in a fit of madness. No one believed in that.

I went. First I had to find appropriate funeral clothing in Pamplona; something black. I finally succeeded, but cursed the small size of Spanish women – nothing seemed to fit. Then I had to leave the next morning from San Sebastian, to where the conference had moved. The other participants seemed a bit stunned at this quick change; they talked about political philosophy and were not familiar with such events as massacres in the parliament.

Early next morning I flew to Heathrow from Bilbao, and from there to Athens where I would catch an old Tupolov to Yerevan. 'Armenian Airlines' the company was called, unknown to all PC screens at Heathrow. I languished there, reading *Figaro* and missing the children, thinking that I should never have said yes to this mission, dangerous as it was. *Figaro* reported that there was an insurrection in Yerevan and shooting in the streets. I called back to the Russian section in the ministry in Oslo. 'What the hell is going on there? Do I need an armed guard or what?' There was nothing going on, they said, according to their cables from Moscow where our embassy was. And security was the responsibility of the host government. And flying Tupolevs was quite safe, as we did that all the time in the Russian federation. But of course, I was in charge, they could only give me advice. But also, being chairman of the OSCE implies that one must at least be present at the funeral at the political level. All the other foreign ministers were coming.

I could have turned and gone back home there at Heathrow, but of course I did not. There had been similar situations before, but perhaps not as dangerous. But I was not going to let the men in that ministry think that I was afraid. Yet I thought about the children: was it right to do this?

In Athens the desk of 'Armenian Airlines' was non-existent, and no one at this Third World airport had heard about the flight to Yerevan. But finally there was a flight announced twice, at two differet gates and at two different desks, going to Yerevan. I picked one, and it was right. It was like a scene from a B movie – I half-expected the passengers to pull their guns. I was sitting in so-called business class, some seats without any numbers in an old rickety plane. The stewardess, whose name I am sure was Ludmila, wrote a paper tag with my seat number – this was before the computer age. Just in order to learn more about the flight, I asked casually: 'Do you fly this route often?', 'Yes, daily every Friday', she replied. I asked no more questions.

I got a stiff drink before take-off – this was all Russian standard – and the rest of the information was in Russian. I practised my prayers, as usual in these kinds of airplanes, remembering that this was not the first time in such a tin box. Luckily there was not much turbulence, and we reached Yerevan at three a.m.

We have no embassy there, so the people from Moscow had come down. It seemed OK. From the hotel I could hear shooting in the streets, and clearly the political elite was numbed by what had happened. Fear was rampant; no one felt safe. The security provided for the foreign guests was nil. The next day we walked behind the open coffins with bloody corpses through the streets of town, and anyone could have done anything. The funeral was grotesque, as the killings had been, and people were in shock. The atmosphere everywhere was tense.

A young diplomat assigned to me was my escort. He wanted to show me what the Armenians are really like. I told him that I was a Christian, too. He lit up, and eagerly showed me their most beautiful churches where the poor, ordinary people were worshipping. I have seldom seen such genuine, intense prayer and such real respect for God. It was absolutely striking, how people in the street are deeply, deeply Christian in Armenia – this forsaken people, isolated geogaphically and persecuted for centuries by their Muslim neighbours. It was crystal clear:

Christ is at the centre of their national life, much more so than in any Western European country. I felt ashamed, as a fellow Christian, that our own states are so indifferent to God. Despite all their suffering and hardship, the Armenians believe unconditionally. How was it possible? Human explanations fall short.

There was a complete contrast between the spirit and calm of the people and the political class, which feared armed rebellion and unrest. I talked with the president and the foreign minister, who both, like by a miracle, had survived. They were afraid, absent-minded, in shock. Later, at the reception for the foreign guests the Canadian foreign minister took me aside. 'You can hitch-hike with me to Norton airbase tonight', he said, 'no need to risk being here any longer.' To enter into his military plane was wonderful. Never have I appreciated a gesture more than this.

Kristiansand

A Sunday in February in Kristiansand, the main town in the south of Norway. I come from these parts. The two youngest children are with me. We are heading for another town on the coast, at the very southern tip of Norway where my parents live. It is the start of winter holidays, and the children will visit their grandparents.

Off the train from Oslo, the crazy winds meet us on the platform. The sea is next to us, and the weather is normal for the season: at least 15 metres per second, oftentimes more. I relish the smell of the salty sea. We bow against the wind and hurry to catch a bus to the final destination.

But no. This is the old puritanical south. There are no buses until later. We have to wait for three hours. 'Let's take a brisk walk', I say, 'and then find a place to eat something.' The children agree, but we soon realise that everything in town is closed: not only shops, but all cafés, restaurants, everything. Not a soul in sight – the town is dead. Carrying the luggage, we proceed towards the town square. The station where we could have deposited the luggage is of course also closed. The wind takes my hat across the square – no one down here wears a hat! Such foolish items are impossible. What you need here is proper rain gear.

The wind is lovely – so much fresh air, feels like being able to fly. The seagulls skriek, and descend on us looking for food. There is absolutely no one in sight on this Sunday morning. We walk around, but the rain comes. 'Why is everything closed?' the children ask. 'This is the south,' I explain, 'here people go to church until 1 p.m., and nothing can open until after church hours.' This is still true in our secularised age. 'Church hour' is a standard term in Norwegian, denoting the time on Sundays when a shop or restaurant may open. And only a few shops are allowed to be open on Sundays. Here this rule is applied to perfection.

We need this difference between days. Imagine the nightmare if every day were a weekday, with the same commercialism and stress! Never having the quiet pensiveness of a Sunday; the time to recollect oneself and have time to reflect on a deeper level. But the pressures are on to abolish Sunday, especially from the forces of the market. They would like to make us all into consumers all the time. That is a life bereft of joy and dignity. As I think about this, the children bring me back to reality: We are outside in what seems to become a small storm and rain, dragging our luggage and having yet more than two hours to wait. 'Where shall we go?' the youngest asks.

'There was no room for them in the inn', it is written in the Gospels. Mary and Joseph found no room in Bethlehem.

There is no comparison of course. What is open today? The churches and the prayer houses, which are all over town. The Catholic church in town is by the harbour, a small red brick building. It was built only a few years ago, and I think to myself that it is near to a miracle that we have a church here where Catholicism is still met with solid prejudice. Catholics are equated with Jesuits, a name only whisperered: they are the cunning and devious Machiavellians, people still think, seeking souls for the Roman Church. I sometimes joke that I wish the Jesuits would live up to their old reputation a bit more today. However, what is interesting here in my home area is that Counter-Reformation prejudices about Catholicism still exist. As a child I remember seeing the first nuns of my life in my home town where the Church for some odd reason possesses a summer retreat house, 'Stella maris'. The nuns were clad in long, black habits, with what seemed to be a hat with big brims. When they occasionally went into town, in pairs, we children were stunned with amazement and fear. They looked like penguins on shore, strange and foreign. We heard that they could not take a bath in the open air, and inspected their retreat house from our rowing boats. Indeed, they had a bath house, an unheard-of thing in our world where we ran around half-naked in the summer season.

Recalling the uninterrrupted prejudices about Catholics since the Reformation in this still very religious part of Norway, I hurried the children with me towards the Catholic church, looking for the tower in the heavy wind and rain. The stormy weather is even tougher in the harbour, but we approach the church and open the door.

Being a small and poor church, the door opens directly from the street into the church. There the priest was conse-crating the bread and wine at that very moment. The wind is forced out and the door closes behind us. Dripping wet, we kneel down.

It is a moment of intense happiness: here I am, I am at home with You. This is where I belong and find my strength to go out again. I am filled with the quiet joy of being in front of the sacrament, seeing the familar red light by the tabernacle, the choir boys kneeling, the smell of incense; but most of all the chalice on the altar. If these things were but things, how could one experience such an inner peace and joy? The contrast between the deso-late street outside and the rough weather and the serenity and intensity inside is striking. I remember how I used to enter into churches in Rome, long before I believed that Christ was inside them. Especially one time in Via del Corso, the noisy, dirty main street in old Rome, where Italians display their childish love for honking the horns and shouting in the traffic; I went into a small, dark, unassuming, even ugly church. Inside it was dark and quiet, only the red light by the Tabernacle and some candles alight. But there was a presence there which I sensed strongly even then. Why else would I remember just that occasion? I stayed there in that deep peace for a long time.

Since then I have found this peace every time I go into a Catholic church. Many times when I am in uproar, or distracted, or simply bored and restless. The peace resides there, even if I often only realise it afterwards. But today the joy was there immediately: Here we are at home, we need nothing more. It could be anywhere, in any town, with unknown people. I come as a stranger, but am no stranger. All of a sudden I am so happy that there is a meaning beyond all the daily trivial things we do – a meaning that is not separate from these things, but which should be at their very centre. I travel on the train with my children; I walk round the town with them looking for a place to be; I take a bus to my parents with them, and we are happy together. Ordinary? Yes, but at the same time extraordinary: I can do these small things with love, to help others, or I can do them because I have to, and they mean nothing to anyone beyond mere duty. They can be devoid of love.

I have often thought that when I give a gift to someone, or do a service to him or her, it is not the gift or service itself that matters. It is the love behind it. There is nothing so moving as the discovery that someone thought about another person, that someone really cared. The money value of the gift has nothing to do with it. Likewise, there is no greater betrayal than giving a gift where no love is behind it.

Could it be that this ordinary life is directly related to Christ? Usually the link is not at all clear – it is as if one lives in two worlds: one where one may find some peace and joy sometimes in the church; another everyday life filled with tasks and duties which often seem completely meaningless. How can the two worlds be reconciled?

It is said that we see 'through a glass, darkly'. But nonetheless we can sense something hopeful which can be explored further: the joy in the church cannot be meant to be outside the real world. I must be able to take that joy and bring it into all that I do, and to thus give it to others. This only seems logical, although I do not yet know how this is really possible.

The children grumble and complain: 'We went to Mass last night and you said it was good for Sunday, and now we want to eat somewhere but you always take us to churches.' I manage to make them interested in a statue of Our Lord with many sheep around him. The sheep look real and bring out the motherly instinct of the youngest child. She forgets to ask for 'proof, now, at once' about the transubstantiation, which she otherwise usually does, for 'no one can make himself invisible and sit inside a biscuit', as she is wont to say in her logical manner.

The congregation is mixed. 'There are fifty nationalities here', says the priest after Mass. I think to myself, 'there are only a hundred people.' Most of them are foreigners. The priest is a Philippino; he recognises me and smiles. There is one more priest, newly ordained, from Norway. He wears a soutane, and is more Roman than the other. They are happy to see me, who acts in a way as a bridge between the Prostestants and the Catholics. The Protestants refuse to invite the Catholics for the ecumenical prayer week. I agree to come later to speak at an ecumencial gathering.

The Catholics are not prominent in town, immigrants as they are. There are one or two Norwegians here, mostly converts. It is hard for foreigners to be accepted here. They have no positions of influence in Norwegian society, and being Catholic does not make matters better. If I can do a little – just a little – to make all Christians realise that the only way forward is ecumenical, I will be content. 'They have no doctrine; that disappeared with Martin Luther', says the Norwegian priest.

I do not comment. Such issues are no longer of any importance. We are living in societies that are rapidly losing any trace of Christianity. That is the issue. Who can afford to criticise each other among Christians? I remember how the apostles quarelled and how St Paul reprimanded them.

In this little community I know that I am one of them, that I belong. This is a bond that transcends all class distinctions, nationality, and educational levels. By such criteria, I have little in common with most people there. It is the love for Christ that unites us, nothing else. We are, mysteriously, engaged in the same endeavour: to love God and to bring Him to others – somehow.

As we leave, what seemed to be a waste of time in Kristiansand on a lonely Sunday morning turned out to be a visit to the well of strength and joy. I understood that it is this joy that can give meaning to all that we do in our everyday lives.

Tromsø

300 kms north of the Polar Circle there is a Carmelite monastery called 'Totus tuus' after the Pope's motto. When he visited Scandinavia in 1989 he also stopped in Iceland, bringing Polish Carmelites with him. Some few years later their numbers had grown because of new vocations, enough for them to make a foundation in Tromsø. Just that is almost an incredible fact.

So twelve Polish nuns came there to build a monastery. They started with no money and their bare hands, much to the surprise of the locals, who had never seen a nun before, even less a contemplative one. They just started to work. Soon the locals were watching, and then someone stole from the building materials that the nuns had stored on their lot.

The locals were shocked and infuriated: how could

anyone steal from poor nuns? The Tromsø men decided to help the nuns build their monastery, as these were some 'hell of real women', as they say, as a fond compliment, in their dialect. The women of Tromsø helped, too, with money.

Soon 'Totus tuus' was ready, among the birches and the snow-clad mountains, facing the sea and the town. Now the Tromsø people felt that this had become their monastery. They were proud of it, not understanding anything about Carmelites or other Catholics. But they knew human depth and love when they met it.

I came to Tromsø, taking a taxi to my hotel. 'Do you want to see our monastery?', the taxi driver asked, not knowing me at all. He made an extra tour to show me the latest pride of the town.

Since then the nuns have had more vocations, now numbering twenty-four; also local women. They made a modest recording of Polish Christmas songs at Christmas 2000. It was nothing special in terms of musicality.

The record topped the lists in Norway all that Christmas. The nuns were the object of newspaper articles and TV programmes. 'Nun-hysteria', one paper had it. The attraction of the silence of 'Totus tuus' was undeniable, also non-Christians came there to experience it.

The wind blows where it will, and you do not know whence it comes.

Kleven

Kleven is the old harbour of my home town Mandal. It has been a port for sailing ships for several centuries due to the good harbour conditions, with deep water. There was also a shipyard there, repairing sailing ships during the winter. Rumour has it that the natives would put out lights by the sea in order to make ships wreck on the dangerous cliffs, thus getting orders for repairs for the winter. For centuries Kleven was a haven not only to sailors, but also to prostitutes and bars. The natives needed to know rudimentary English; in my childhood still remembered as 'Kleve-English'.

When I was a little girl, we rowed or sailed from Kleven to our summer house nearby. So I was familiar with the place, picturesque now as then; with skippers' white houses and sailors' more modest cabins. But because it was a port, with many boats in the bay, it still had a somewhat tainted reputation. It was not high class to be from there.

I had been at home for a day last winter when I heard that Bjarne was dead. He was my best fisherman friend. He had just turned seventy-seven, and I was profoundly sad at his death. If anyone lived in harmony with God and nature, it was Bjarne. He was, like his father and father's father before him, a fisherman. This was a really honourable trade. Each morning at dawn one could hear his boat; a typical fishing boat from the region; wooden, hand-made, about twenty-seven feet in length. He would visit his 'places', that is, where the fish and crab waited. They were his places; no one but stupid tourists would try to put their nets there. Everyone local respected the places each fisherman had, often inherited from their fathers.

When I was a little girl in the summer house, I woke up to the sound of Bjarne's motor boat on the fiord. It was a sure sign of morning. In all kinds of weather you could see him in the boat, standing erect at the tiller. He lived, of course, from the fishing, and systematically harvested the catch. His sons have also become fishermen.

As I left town as an adult, I lost the childhood memory of his daily routine. But when I came back to visit with my own children, I reopened the contact, for he provided us with crabs every year. I would call him once I got home: 'Bjarne, could you take my boys to sea to teach them some fishing?' 'How are the crabs now? Is it too early to find them full?' I would take the children to Kleven to collect live crabs, a ritual and a feast. Bjarne always had full crabs – they were caught in his traps, and then kept there and fed with his fish until they were full of white and red crab meat. The biggest crabs were no good, they were seldom full of meat; the medium to small ones were fine. We would sit on his pier, pulling up the crab traps, and look at all the crabs crawling over one another. The children cried with fear and excitement. Then we would pick out the ones we wanted, carefully holding them up by the shell only so as not to have fingers destroyed, put them in a big box and listen to the sizzling sound they make on land.

At home we would cook them, killing them quickly by dumping them into boiling water, but first the children would let them out on the kitchen floor, screaming with excitement. I told Bjarne how some American animal-lovers were our guests, and how they were shocked at this 'barbarism'. 'What are they saying?', they asked me when they heard the sizzling sound. 'They say: save the whales', I replied. Bjarne laughed in his quiet way: he could not understand how anyone could have such an unnatural relationship with nature as modern urbanites. He had more respect for nature than any of them. He was part of it.

Now Bjarne has left us, as silently as he lived. Death was also completely natural to him. He was a deep Christian; not intellectual, not learned, but with great respect for learning. He was proud of all my travels and of my 'accomplishments', but he was unaware that he perhaps had reached a closeness to God that most of us never will. For him, the unity of life was simpy the way things were: man lived from nature, which is God's gift to man; and man thanks his God every day for this gift. I am sure that he went to meet Christ with the same naturalness as he went about fixing his fishing equipment. Therefore I am not sad for him, but for those of us who will never again be able to sit in the boat with him, talking about the strange ways of these urban Oslo tourists and of all the problems people on land – called 'land crabs' in our dialect – create for themselves.

Bjarne was full of silent virtue – another concept he did not know. God was in Kleven through him; that much is certain.

CHAPTER 6

'VOIR LA VIE AUTREMENT'

Travelling by train in France; I noticed posters in the stations for recruitment to the famous Foreign Legion. 'Voir la vie autrement' , the slogan read: 'to see life differently' . Indeed, one needs to see life differently if one contemplates joining the Foreign Legion's tough professional forces; a life far away from the amenities of comfortable modern living.

But this slogan stayed with me, because it denotes what the Christian must decide to do and indeed renew the will to do over and over again. It is far from a one-time decision.

Christianity offers an entirely different way of life to that of most people today. This is a supranatural reality which one can only 'see' if one makes a real effort, but this is possible for everyone. Once you know something of this surpranatural life – which you only know in glimpses in this life – you will ultimately be dissatisfied if you turn your back on it, despite its demands .

The mere possibility of such a 'different way of life' is a surprise to most, and it is not easy to understand what the Christian way of life is. One discovers it as one walks it. But in fact, one can speak of two mutually exclusive ways of life:

The way most people see life is as a continous succession of experiences without any deeper meaning than enjoying comfort and getting by. But there is a reality that is different; a reality that is the very make-up, the plan for human life. In the beginning of one's Christian life one experiences the emptiness of the superficial way of life, and one seeks something else. Later on there is more knowledge of this other way, but one never sees it clearly. Yet the surest sign one has is the recognition of the emptiness of the life on the surface of things; perhaps one could say, the life of things, not of love.

Christ's presence in our lives and in the world is a mystery. If we seek something beyond the superficial, we may find Christ. To the one who seeks, there is a promise of finding what one seeks. This time is one of such seeking: whereas many people are completely taken up by things and live like beasts, as the ancients would say, with no refinement or virtue; many others see that this way of life is degrading to the human being, and seek a better way. They may never have heard about Christianity, but they know in themselves that the human being is destined for something greater and more noble than consumerism and materialism. They seek virtue for themselves, a word almost forgotten. Our time is one of extreme materialism, but also one of great dissatisfaction with this. Christianity is increasingly replaced by a completely secular culture, but there is also a growing search for spiritual values. I think these times are much like the end of the Roman Empire in this respect.

The greatness of ordinary life, a wonderful term indeed. This is the core of our lives: we live them in ordinary circumstances, and they seem so dull, so boring, so insignificant, so useless. Days seem to follow one another and we seem to accomplish nothing at all: going to work, getting tired, trying to make a good life for the children, seeing old age approaching, getting older ourselves, then perhaps dying suddenly or after a long, painful struggle. What is great about such a life? Nothing to be remembered by – just one more human being in a long chain, soon forgotten by everybody. All the things you had acquired – 'you bring nothing with you when you go', as the Dutch-Swedish singer Cornelis Wreesvijk sang. Those you loved, even those you loved, you have to leave. Or they leave you.

Too often Christians lead a kind of double life. This ordinary life which they think means nothing and which they live as a duty, but which is not at the very centre of their Christian life; and then the life of Christian consolation, as I call it; going to Mass and enjoying the company of other 'like-minded' on Sunday and holidays. But this is entirely wrong, because you cannot live such a double life. You have only one life: the here and now, your ordinary life. And that ordinary life is meant to be great, because God has called you before you even were born, and has a plan for your life. Indeed, this life is great, but you have to discover it.

This is of course a tremendous suggestion; and one that is so amazing that one can hardly believe it. It means, if you take it seriously for a moment and consider, that you can be doing God's work wherever you are, in every circumstance, and that He needs you to do this work in order to make the world better. That would mean that you can live a full, 'divine' life, attuned to the will of God in the here and now, and that your life will 'count' insofar as you live it in closeness to God. It would not be the 'heroic' acts that everybody sees that would matter, but the way you live and love God in your own life.

This is a revolutionary change in how one sees life. It is truly representing a turnaround from the way we usually judge when we see others: poor this or that person, no important status in society, no important job, quite ordinary, nothing to admire, he or she has no riches and no power. Then we think that those with status and fame are the ones that really can do things. But when you take away the glitter, those people are often pathetic specimens. You can see life from an entirely human point of view, and most of us do for most of the time. Then only the extraordinary are the signposts, and the ordinary is just filling in the days.

What is this other way of seeing life? How can it be the real way when what we see as ordinary seems to be the reality, just as it is in empirical terms? The other way can be seen when we are open to God and actually spend time in getting to know Him.

I have a friend from Saigon who is now a cardinal, but being a cardinal is probably the least important aspect about him. He would never be interested in having such an august rank. He used to be a prisoner for the sake of his Christian faith. For thirteen years he was in prison; nine of them in solitary confinement. He said that in this situation he could either go crazy, or he could trust in God; really believe that God had a plan for him and that God would take care of him. He was humble enough to do the latter. And clearly God had a plan with the cross this man had to carry: he has become one of the most impressive witnesses to the faith of our time.

The point here is however this; my friend was deprived of every human and societal support. He was certain he was going to die, and that there was never to be a way out of prison for him. His case was utterly hopeless from a human point of view. So he abandoned himself to God, trusting completely in Him.

But we are not usually faced with such stark choices; we simply go on 'limping on both feet' and never make up our minds to trust in God and to try to see life differently. Therefore we never manage to see life differently either. It is enough to really make the effort, and the aid will be given. But the reluctance to so doing is great. Christianity demands a constant effort, and a sacrifice. There are few who are willing to really undertake to try this.

The Right Perspective

Someone once wrote an article entitled 'Ought humans to live in Norway?' The author's conclusion, tongue-in-cheek, was no. The weather is harsh, cold and it is dark almost all year apart from late spring and summer, and the topography consists of mountains and fiords. The fiords are so steep that the few inhabitants often build farms several hundred metres up the steep mountainside where they nest like eagles, and the mountain plateaux are at about 1000 metres and more, which make them uninhabitable for both man and beast. Only four per cent of the land mass of Norway is arable. But, as the joke goes, some strange specimen followed the ice as it melted during the ice age and ended up here.

No one in his right mind would opt to live here, the article argues – one has to be born here to stay. But those who love the toughness of nature, to be tried and tested against nature's powers, want to come. There is much sense in that. When the noise and superficiality of the city is left behind, down in the valley, one reaches freedom and rediscovers human dignity in the mountains.

The Norwegian mountains: stone on stone; barren yet beautiful. And dangerous if one is unprepared. But these waste mountain ranges offer something more than nature untouched: they offer an immense stillness before God. It is a strange experience, but it is a real one. Hiking, hour after hour, in the awesome panorama where a human being is like a frail insect puts a new perspective on oneself in relation to creation.

At first there is the awe and fear.

We were, the whole family, going to hike in one of the highest mountain ranges, Jotunheimen. It is a massif at 1700–2000 metres altitude; not alpine, but a waste plateau with high peaks and stones, stones, stones. Only reindeer moss and some strangely beautiful flowers can grow at this altitude. The stones make it painful to walk unless you have solid boots. The sound of stones falling is all you hear, as you step on them and inadvertently displace them. And then the wind, a constant companion, strong and monotonous. When you pass a sheltering peak, the stillness is surprising, and you want to stop and sit there, comforted by nature itself.

The hike we wanted to make started by a lake, the Gjendin, which is devilish green. The green colour comes from the melted water from the surrounding glaciers. On both sides of the lake there are steep mountainsides that are black, somewhat greyish, with long stripes of water falling down into the lake like a bride's long veil, only colder, more stern. All this ice water comes from numerous glaciers, small and large, scattered in the mountains of Jotunheimen. The name literally means 'home of the jotner', who were monster creatures in Viking mythology. One can imagine them throwing stones at each other for play – and the stones fell down awkwardly, making up the wasteland of huge blocks of stone that characterise this area.

The Gjendin lake is imposing; the mountains even more so. It is really cold up here at 1100 metres. It is in the middle of July, but we need wool caps, mittens, and wind breakers. Being on the lake is a foretaste of the mountains, way up on the sides. I suddenly understand why Norwegians only hike in the mountains in August. It is because this is the time of year when most snow has melted and it is warmest up here. But warm here means that one can be lucky and have sun, while one must know that it will most certainly snow on the same trip.

Our hike starts the next morning. The children are waiting for the crossing of the famous Gjendin-ridge, a steep peak where there is a small path where one has to climb very carefully, step by step; and where one looks down straight into the Gjendin lake – 1700 metres below in a direct line; and if one dares to look down on the other side, it is 600 metres down into the Bess lake.

This climb was made world famous in the first act of Henrik Ibsen's *Peer Gynt*, where Peer boasts to his mother that he rode a reindeer over the ridge and down into the lake: 'Reindeer from above and reindeer from below meet in the same moment', he says – in Norwegian, a fantastic verse with great musicality, 'Rein fra oven, rein fra unden, stansede i same stunden'. We envisage without difficulty the splash of Peer's reindeer as it meets its mirror image, 1700 metres down into the lake.

This literary masterpiece was inspired by this very climb we are making, but which Ibsen himself never made. Crossing the ridge is in the middle of an eight-hour hike, and is described by the Norwegian Tourist Association in its old-fashioned and conservative language as 'somewhat airy'. This was, I was to learn, a grave understatement. There was not one of us who was not afraid when we climbed the last part of the sharp ridge, thanking God that it was only snowing and not blowing too hard. But it was the high point of the trip for the children – something exciting and dangerous; a deed to talk about afterwards. A challenge from nature, not commercial, just awesome in a way they had never experienced before. 'I am afraid', the youngest said. I climbed behind her. 'Don't look down, concentrate on where you put you feet, grip carefully', I said.

There is something noble and extremely satisfactory about man's interaction with nature in this way. One has to use all faculties, mental and physical. One cannot let fear overcome intelligence and skill. One has to learn how to survive, and to use one's abilities. It is a real test, nothing articifical. I understand very well all those who seek challenges in nature – too extreme and dangerous sometimes, but the principle is right: One should test oneself. 'Why do you climb so much?' a journalist asked a Norwegian philosophy professor, also a well-known climber; Arne Næss. 'It is you who have stopped climbing', he replied, 'it is natural to man.'

But most of a mountain hike is not climbing, but walking. This is where one can discover something very important about life.

In the beginning one may talk to the others in the group. After all, one usually walks in a party. But after some hundred metres upwards, there is no more talking. The energy spent on conversation is a waste, and one has quite enough to think about: carrying a backpack of fifteen kilos, watching where one puts one's feet, and getting into a rhythm that is natural for the body.

Once the talking ends, the thinking begins. One sees the awesome, dangerous, and deeply impressive landscape. One is a guest in this place where only reindeer survive. There is no vegetation but the few flowers and the moss which feed the reindeer. They somehow live by this nourishment, which grows by only 0.1 mm each year. The reindeer tracks can be seen, but the animals themselves are shy, smelling human beings at once if the wind is their way. Sometimes one sees them at a far distance, in herds of several thousand. The annual hunting is difficult.

You walk on, minding your step. To the left there is the large Memuru glacier, like a white cape draped around black peaks. It can be traversed, but you need a guide and ropes. My father told me how he hiked here, at least fifty years ago. A couple wanted to cross the glacier, and were told to find a guide. They were stupid, and set off alone. The husband fell into a crevasse. The wife returned for help. But one does not survive for long in that cold. He was dead upon their return.

To the right is the dark Besshøe peak, uninviting, frightening as one approaches: stones on stones, black and grey, and then the snow. All the colours here are shades of black, white and grey – it is snow and stones; stones and snow. Nothing else – yes, a little flower here and there, and then the rein moss, but no life that we can see. There are other animals, and birds, eagle and raven, but this landscape is nonetheless so bare and imposing. It is formed in the ice age; the ice has worked the stone.

What does a little human being do up here? It is a sensible question, for Norwegians never hiked in the mountains until this century. Why should they risk their lives to do that? Nothing to gain, no arable land; nothing but snow, ice and discomfort. It was only when the English aristocracy discovered mountain climbing that Norwegians started to appreciate their vast treasure; the major part of their country.

Without proper clothing and equipment, one takes a risk never to be taken. A fragile human life cannot withstand these forces of nature. In the mountains, like at sea, the weather changes abruptly. A storm appears without notice. When it hits, even in summer, there is no direction to be had and no shelter to be found unless one is prepared. One has always to be alert.

Down in the valley we feel so safe, and even more so in the city. There is seemingly no danger to our physical lives, and we are completeley self-sufficient. We do not even reflect on fear and possible death. We are in full control.

But this is a great illusion. We are not in control, not even of our physical lives. They are taken away when we least expect it, by accidents, sudden illness, or by premature deaths. We are equally surprised each time, and suppress the thought of death at once – at least that of our own death.

The city lulls us into a false sense of personal security. We are seldom afraid and do not know anything about our own physical and psychological limits. We really think we can control our lives to perfection, and arrange them down to the last details. This false sense of security acts like a mental barrier to God. We do not need Him and we do not seek Him. Only when personal disaster strikes, such as the death of someone close, or serious illness, do we suddenly remember the possibility that God may exists after all, and turn to Him like some kind of last resort. As Pascal said, it is better to make a bet that He is alive just in case it were true. When you are dead it is too late to change your mind. After all, there is no cost involved: if God exists, you included Him while still on earth; if He is fiction, then you lost nothing more than the trouble of few prayers.

But who wants to be treated like this? God who loves man and constantly seeks Him is forgotten, and only remembered when there is no other choice. This is how most people treat God today.

He comes in handy when crisis hits. But in all the ordinary, everyday life we are in control and do not need Him, and consequently do not seek Him. If we were more dependent on nature, like in high mountains or at sea, we would realise that we are not in control of our physical survival, and least of all, the survival of our soul. In nature we at least take precautions and act wisely, for we know that we cannot be guaranteed to survive. A storm comes in seconds, an avalanche surprises us, the boat has engine trouble or we fall overboard. We have to be alert in order to avoid disaster, but preparedness and alertness do not in themselves vouch for survival.

In the comfort of the city we are not even alert or prepared; we are simply assuming that we are safe from damage and death. Thus we are as far from God as we can be, for the first step towards Him is to realise that we depend on Him like children. God the Father, we as His children: this is a reality that overshadows everything else. My old Benedictine friend used to say always: 'Remember that God is greater than your heart.'

In the mountains you are constantly aware of your own vulnerability and the limits of your control. You are alert all the time: is there a storm looming? Is fog coming? Do we have the compass and map ready? In winter, do we have the necessary equipment for digging a cave? And at sea, is the wind hardening? Are we too near land? Is the boat going steady? All these things are within our control, and we must know them and use them, otherwise we are not alerted.

But beyond this little control that we human beings can have if we use all our knowledge and faculties, there are vast powers of nature: storms, cold, crevasses, avalanches, fog, roaring white waves that topple your little boat despite all your precautions. In such a natural habitat you learn to see the limits of your own powers. Then you naturally turn to God, and put Him in the right perspective. If you live close to nature, you know what fear is. You will have experienced your own weakness and indeed nothingness when you have encountered nature's enormous might.

Walking on, I see these things more clearly than in the city. It is so deserted and quiet, only the wind is to be heard. The stones are dead and grey. They have been here for ages, and will be so long after I am gone. I am just passing by; the landscape is permanent. The glaciers move, some inches day by day, but one cannot see it. Nature lives – the rein moss grows, but slowly. This landscape is deserted, much like what I imagine the moon surface to be like: stones, peaks, no life in sight. There are none of the amenities of the city. I must survive on what I carry in my rucksack and hope that there will be no storm or fog.

After a while however one feels extremely comfortable. The hiking is easy when the body has found its rhythm. The silence is blissful. In the city the noises take over the mind, and a sudden silence there leads to restlessness. Here in this silence however is peace of mind. Like a bird, one can look down on the city in the depth in the valley. One sees things in perspective, a bird's-eye view of the life down there. Then the thought is very clear; God is present all the time and we do not see Him, for we are taken up by the noises, the superficiality and the activism we so easily engage in. We are busy, but accomplishing little; we are active, but what is it we are doing? Does it last more than a day? Is it going to last for eternity?

The thought of God and God's perspective is frightening for someone who habitually rushes about, filling the days with tasks that have no divine logic to them. Can all these everyday tasks be filled with, or rather, be what they are meant to be, acquire their original meaning in God's plan? Can they be 'divined' and sanctified?

This is a fantastic prospect – how much that would change the world, the city; but even more so, how much that would change you and me, who live our lives in the busy city. The sea and the mountain is not where we have our lives; unlike some forefathers who lived from nature and stayed in nature. We must live in the modern, noisy, busy city. How can such a life be filled with God?

While there, being caught up in business and activism, it seems almost impossible. I have disclosed my own superficial activism hundreds of times: starting the day without a thought of the divine perspective, of God's perspective on these activities and tasks; continuing throughout the day, doing this or that, doing much, hurrying to and fro, and when evening falls, saying a little prayer, too tired for much reflection or hindsight. Then the next day, the same procedure, I have so much to do; no time for prayer or thinking, maybe tomorrow or at the weekend. Yes, on Sunday I will reserve some time for God.

This merry-go-round continues for weeks until one stops to realise the emptiness. One has to return to the

Father's house, to find the right track again. But all those who do not know Him at all do not know what to do or where to go. They just go on like before.

On the mountain trail it is the stillness that makes me reflect deeply. At first I just enjoy the panorama and the physical well-being of getting comfortably warm, feeling the muscles work, relishing the rhythm of walking. Then I realise that this stillness brings me closer to God than most of my everyday life. Up here I can talk with Him so easily. I can really sink into the depth of my soul, penetrate the superficiality. There is nothing to take the peace away.

This is of course what the contemplatives have always known: solitude and silence allow you to pray and adore God. There is no surprise in any of this. But only now do I fully realise how absolutely vital this depth, this immersion in God is to our lives. In the mountains I can literally see this city life from the bird's-eye perspective. I imagine that this is how God sees our lives – He has the overview we lack. But not only Him: we also have to see our lives in a supernatural perspective. It is difficult, but it is necessary, lest we lose the point of it all.

In the city we think that this or that action or accomplishment is important simply because human logic tells us so. Be powerful, famous, successful – yes, that is good. Add some pious prayers and a dash of Christianity, and you are surely saved. Then live long and have a good old age until you unfortunately have to die at some point. But first, attain all the security and safety you can. We are all like this, more or less. We tend to judge everything we do in our own, human perspective. We have no idea how God sees things most of the time because we do not strive to see things in His perspective.

That is why so much activity is futile and sterile, and we only discover this when we are exhausted by our own lack of depth and perspective. Therefore we should seek the stillness of nature more often, or that of the monastery.

On my hike I saw all this clearly. God's perspective on things is the real one, and mine is a distorted one. Up here I could appreciate the divine perspective, meditating on all this. I saw how *die Schwerpunkt* lies in God, not in us, and that gave me an immense joy and peace of mind. Up here it was all clear to me. But what about the life in the city? How could I maintain the divine perspective there?

I think most people have had these clear moments. Some have them in nature's church; others in a retreat, and yet others when they face a severe crisis in life. But the insight is just the beginning. The key is to keep to the realism you have discovered.

I have gradually learnt that the norms of piety, as they are called – the ways to maintain a presence of God throughout the day – are as necessary as fresh air. If you live by the human logic alone, your actions are so sterile. Only when you offer an action to God, as a service to Him out of love, will you have the ability to love the persons you meet or work with. Only then will they see Christ, at least a touch of Him, in you. By yourself you can do nothing, however competent your actions be.

We should expose our limits more often in order to see how dependent we are on God, like children who think they can manage on their own, but who fall and have to be helped. And once we realise this, we must cling to the realism we have discovered. It is of vital importance to retain the supernatural perspective in our everyday lives, otherwise nothing is gained and not all the activity is able to be transformed by God. In the city, the only way is constant conversation with the Father. Our task is much more difficult than that of monastics, I dare say. But the means are available to us.

I was thinking back, how I had been helped on the way by God, in His graces, in making Himself present when I least expected it, in the Dominican garden in Oslo in 1981, in Pannonhalma in 1992, and in lesser ways later. Despite all this it took me a long time to acquire a little – just a little – of the supernatural perspective. But once I discovered this possibility, my ordinary life started to change.

Seeing Life Differently: Ordinary Work

My job as state secretary came to an abrupt end in March 2000 when the government was ousted by the Socialists. I had by then been in that position for about three years, almost always travelling and working late. It had been a continuous struggle between being a mother and a politician, and the family had clearly been neglected. The trips abroad – about once or twice a week – were a big burden on the children. I tried to juggle it, but there was no solution with such a job. So I was relieved when it ended, because it was clear to me that the children missed me so much when I was away. When a mother is away, it is harder on the children than when the father is away. This is my experience, although many women will not like to hear this.

But when the government fell, I also lost all my privileges. I had had a secretary, a personal assistant, a driver, an elegant office, a position next to the foreign minister. In the ministry, made up of 1,400 people I always had a group working for me: writing my speeches, arranging my trips, escorting me here or there. Then there was the constant press attention to a government of which I formed a part; the challenges and the ability to make decisions and to be a policy maker in the middle of international politics. All this I loved dearly; a lot of vanity of course crept into this, but a lot of the work was also plainly exciting for someone who had studied international politics, but not practised it in an important position. I hated to be away from the family and I had longed for more intellectual work, for time to write, but at the same time I loved the challenge of acting and doing, of being in the middle of the 'heat'. Most of all I liked to work with all the professional people in the foreign ministry; to make strategy and to discuss tactics.

When a government falls, all this changes overnight. One leaves one's job and office immediately, after some days of transition until the next government is in place. It is really sad to leave one's friends and colleagues, those with whom one has worked intensely for a long time. The government team is dispersed and will never convene again. It is a time of great sorrow that only those who have experienced it, can understand.

I returned to the University of Oslo where I had a professorship in international politics. This was in a way as close as one could be to the ministerial work, but it was entirely different. It was not operative, but only analytical. I had no privileges any more, and sat on the sidelines of events. I felt tremendously restless and bored, and could not find my place. Now I suddenly had the time I had wanted with the children, which was good, but I was very unhappy in professional terms. I missed the work of politics, despite all the tiredness and long trips, and although I did not want to go back, I was dissatisfed with the university. It was an ivory tower, far removed from the real world. I did not want to return to studying politics after having been a policy maker, but I did like the chance to write again.

This time of being thrown out of office, and suddenly having to rely only on oneself was a useful one from the point of view of Christianity. I had become so used to service from others and a programme of work that others set for me that I did not really have to examine what I was doing. A lot of it was naturally representation; useful perhaps, but superficial. A lot was also press appearances that were equally superficial – again, perhaps useful, but nothing that left a lasting impression on anyone. Then there was my own vanity: I liked all these performances so much. I loved a debate on direct TV which I usually won; I just loved the fight, and could go on with that. But was it really of any importance?

I knew that I had a talent for writing and a vocation to write, and was in theory happy to be back to a situation where I could do something more serious than travelling from meeting to meeting, going from dinner to lunches to receptions, being in radio and TV debates where the intellectual challenge was nil, and you would win if you knew just a little more than the journalist, which posed no problem at all.

But when you are stripped of all your usual support systems, you see yourself more as you really are. I had a topic for a book and even a publisher, so I should ideally just sit down and be happy to get on with it. But I could not. I kept wondering why God had left me in this modest office, in a quiet place, without people around to team up with. I was profoundly unable to see His will in this, and to concentrate on the moment and on the present day.

If I had really been trusting in Him, I would not have reacted like this. But even if we believe, we are not saints. We are always very human and should be very human, but we must learn, again and again, to be humble. So I was slow to learn that I had to trust in God.

Being so dissatisfied with my academic ivory tower, I decided to create my own portfolio: I started to work for an international consultancy firm, worked for an operative foreign policy institute, and wrote columns in several papers. I also continued to be the head of the Christian Democratic Party's Foreign Policy Committee. But I still had to learn to work on my own, not relying on anyone else.

This meant that I could not easily escape from myself. My main job was the professorship, and I needed to write a book about military intervention in the Balkans. That in turn meant that once I entered my office at the university in the morning, I had the day's programme laid out before me: write the book. I was also teaching, but the main task was the writing. I could not escape from myself: I would either write, or stare at the wall. I could not escape the difficulty of writing by doing something else.

How does one do such a thing when one lacks inspiration? To write is a lonely process, and most of the time one lacks inspiration. To do other jobs is also a lonely pursuit: being a housewife, to take one example. One does the housework that is only noticed when it is NOT done. Likewise, one works with the thousand and one details of child care, and no one is there to appreciate it.

Self-discipline is not needed when you have others around you to make your programme. My secretary used to write a weekly list, filled with meetings. I could just do one thing after the other, not having to think too much. The day was filled, and more than that. Some of it was demanding, but my 'support systems', the routines, made up for much of it. Now, on the other hand, I had to be creative and self-disciplined; otherwise I would know it myself right away.

My work now demanded much more initiative and self-discipline than before. It was not easy. I sometimes climbed up the walls in my all-too-quiet office. The telephone rang seldomly compared to before and, as I had no official status, all the contacts who had wanted to see me because they could get money or political support out of it, were gone. I suffered from what someone jokingly, but correctly, has called 'Limousine-Abstinence'.

On the other hand, now I could see how much of my former job had been travel and meetings without any deeper content. I am sure diplomacy is important; but it is also a self-perpetuating system. One could do away with a lot of international meetings and no one would ever know the difference.

I got started on my writing and teaching; on my writing for the papers and on my consulting. I was my own master; I was free. That was good from a family point of view, as well as from the point of view of being free to write about important issues without having to take careful political concerns into account. But from a purely human point of view I had to be much more self-disciplined and careful in planning what I would do each day. So I started a rather tough regime, knowing that either I would follow a schedule and work hard whatever the circumstances, or I would not be able to work at all. No one would 'punish' me if I did not.

Again, from the purely human point of view it was very good to have time for the children. I had not realised how much they had suffered when I had been away. They had been good about it; and I had sublimated it. Now I clearly saw how much they needed me and my time. The time was essential: to come home in the afternoon at set times and have dinner with them; to help them with homework and play and talk. The family is becoming even more important at a time when society is breaking down in so many ways.

But only now, when I did put the priority on the children before my other job, did I understand how absolutely vital this work is. Usually you repress it, because you have other commitments and you do not want to admit the pain of being away from the children and of not having time for them. But when you finally allow youself to be honest, you see what it is really about. Being father and mother is much more and of a different order than anything else. It is where you can learn to love, because your children depend on you and only you in this life. They ask you to be everything to them. You must protect them, teach them, and be with them, charged with making them into full and virtuous human beings. This is done through much work and much love. They reminded me of the little boy in Kosovo who had wanted to be loved.

Work well: The First Key

The ordinary life is the place we are. It is either a place we are by haphazard chance, by a kind of 'failure' on the part of God, or it is a place of insignificance and devoid of meaning, and we do right in wishing we were somewhere else. The success of life then comes when we are famous, rich, or significant in the eyes of the world.

'Do I really believe that God has a plan for my life here in Norway?' I asked myself. It seemed completely useless to be there, with nothing Catholic at all about life, and rather a hostility that made Christianity seem out of place. Why should I spend my life there? It was easy to be Catholic and Christian among other 'like-minded', but it was seemingly impossible in this place. The surroundings were quite pagan.

Later I came to love this fact and count myself lucky to be Christian in such a place. This is because I have found what my friend must have already known for a long time;

viz. that the fountain of faith is inside you. You do not
need favourable circumstances at all, in fact, the words of
St Paul are deeply true: 'When I am weak, I am strong'. For
those who look for 'empirical' proof, as we all do from
time to time, this is interesting. The ones that believe do it
in spite of the persecutions and indifference of the environment.

I could visit Rome and be a tourist, feeling empty and
superficial. The place was not the key. The fountain of life
– the nourishment for the faith – was not in the place or in
customs, people, or tradition. The 'support system', as I
call it, was in the sacraments and in personal prayer; in
keeping up a conversation with God under all circumstances; good and bad.

Christ was not to be found in specific places, but in me
and in other people. It was necessary to have access to the
sacraments, but nothing more. The rest was up to me. If I
let myself go astray through negligence, which I did again
and again, I had to find the way back through the sacraments and prayer. I started to realise more and more that
real life, reality, was vested in this 'connection' with
Christ; not in anything societal or geographical. This realisation is the beginning of real life in Christ, in 'seeing life
differently'. This inner life, as it is called, is the very basis
for the 'outer' life which everyone can observe.

But we are not angels, and we do not spend daily life in
prayer in a church. We are normal people with a lot of
work to do all the time. This material reality is also given,
and takes up most of our time and our lives. I had overcome the dualism of faith vs. life; but how did life itself
and all its work become imbued with Christianity?

The incarnation must mean that Christ is present in the
world all the time, also in material reality, not only in
people. We are not only in an individual, personal relationship with Christ, but the mission implies bringing
Him to others, and also to 'incarnate' Him in the structures
of the world – politics, economics, families, the work
place. Unless this is possible, Christianity becomes a solip-
sistic affair for the lucky ones that find Christ for

themselves. That is not what Christian solidarity is about, or Christian love. The whole world can become transformed into being good and just, but it all depends on the cooperation of human beings with God. We were created with free will, and can choose non-cooperation.

Here the full meaning of the concept of *vocation* enters. It is really about being what one is created for; becoming, finding one's place, *existentially* and in fact, *ontologically*. It is not a trade or a profession, but about *being* fully what one should be. This is the happiness which life in Christ brings; it is becoming what one's potential is. God's plan for each human person is unique, as He knows us individually by name. This is a fact so radical and breathtaking that one is numbed by it.

The vocation is then the fullness of what each one is intended to be. I have often thought about this as the gradual self-knowledge we get in life. I used to think so much about my *place*: What was I supposed to be doing? Professionally, in public life, in private life? In other words, where was my place, the place where I really belonged?

In God's perspective this must be clear, but even if I could see things a little from His perspective now, I was still as much in the dark. For many years I had known that my place, my vocation, what I was and am in my deeper self, was to be someone who wrote and worked in the interface between politics and academia, someone who sought to bring Christian norms into society, and most of all, someone who was a mother.

I gradually realised that all these elements made up my vocation. The way I realised this, was retrospectively: when looking back, I saw a consistency in pursuing the question of politics and ethics, of how to study and analyse politics in order to have an impact on society, not in order to stay in an ivory tower. My many years of stalemate between an academic and a politically active profession was never going to be resolved, because I finally had understood that I was bridging the two worlds.

My college professor in the States who once urged me to

become a medieval scholar had been very wrong in his escapist views of the world. Luckily I had resisted then, because I knew that this was not for me. I loved the scholarship, but hated, really detested, the ivory tower. I wanted influence in the middle of the world, to have an impact. So political science, and not philosophy, was for me. Aristotle had rightfully named it the 'highest practical science'. Much later, when I became state secretary of foreign affairs, I had loved that immensely because I could effect changes and wield influence. But after some years I missed the ability to analyse and write, to go deeper. So now I was back to that again. But I knew that my professional vocation was to be in both worlds.

To know for me was rooted not only in the experience of this persistent and consistent interest, but also in a deeper certitude we have about what is right for us. In many situations I felt, after a while, that 'this is not really me'. I think this is how we know about vocation, through this inner certitude. 'This is what I am made to do', 'This is what I can identify with', and so on. It is a gradual realisation.

Work, all that we do in ordinary life, is the venue for changing both ourselves, others, and the world itself.

In a secular perspective, working well is the way to happiness and satisfaction. It is the place for personal development. I have never understood those who prefer idleness: it is the most destructive situation for any human being. 'Idleness is the root of all evil', a saying goes. This puts it starkly, but truly. I see many idle people around me in Norway; not for lack of jobs, but for lack of will and initiative. Many, many receive state aid and get by as well on that as on wages. When young, able people are unemployed by their own will, I react strongly. It is awful not to work, a tragedy for those who are involuntarily unemployed, but morally speaking it is much worse for those who are too lazy to take a job. I cannot imagine spending the days without working, wasted for ever. How can anyone stand it?

Then I also fail to understand those who desire early

retirement unless it is for health reasons. Many I know take to Spain to live on the Costa del Sol. Fine for a day or two, but for good? Just sit in the sun and do nothing? It seems an utter horror, a waste of potential and fruitfulness. The low pension ages in Europe are also a mystery to me. I think it is a terrible prospect to retire at sixty unless one has to, for various reasons.

But work is more than paid work, and one can always find ways to work. The key to finding meaning in work must first of all be that it is done well, as perfectly as humanely possible. That is plain common sense: sloppy, shoddy work is disgusting in human terms. It does not give you satisfaction, and it does no good to anyone. It is just a waste of time.

But work well done is really satisfactory. The joy of having accomplished something, of having made an effort, of having spent oneself in the process, gives more satisfaction than other things in life. It need not be sophisticated work at all: I am very content and happy when I do the housework well, making the home a pleasant place to be for all of us. When one is sloppy and superficial in one's work, it is such a personal defeat: you know that you have done less than what you can do, and you are secretly ashamed of your own laziness and lack of ambition. I have this tendency to want quick results and sometimes not to take the time to make the necessary effort, getting bored easily. It is really a lack of perseverance. My father, on the contrary, has always worked with the greatest care and finished everything to the last detail. I see the difference in humility even though he is not a Christian, whereas I claim to be one.

Then comes the sheer usefulness of good and hard work. It improves the world. There is human progress in almost all fields; what is lacking today is an ethical framework, not improvements in technology. The food production of the world could easily feed the world's population if it were more justly managed, and medicine could be available to all with an effort at redistribution. All this has happened thanks to human work.

But above all good work develops the person. It is where you can develop in virtue. You improve in skills, intellectually, professionally, and you mature in your way of working. There is a joy of working, like there is a joy of learning: you use your capacity as a human being. I love my work because it poses challenges, and it gives satisfaction when I meet those challenges.

The first key to finding Christ in one's work must surely be that it is done well in purely human terms.

Work as Service: The Second Key

But working well can be done without any other consideration than simply getting a good result and getting satisfaction out of it, both personally and in terms of money. I know many, many people who work hard and well in order to advance and to make as much money as possible. It is good to be ambitious, but it has to directed at something. The intention is the major issue here.

As a mother I can more easily understand how work can be service, and why it becomes changed when it has the right intention. I looked in some old albums the other day: the children were so small, yet it didn't seem to be long ago. How much work it all was! I had forgotten about all that, but when I saw the pictures of the four small ones dressed up nicely, two of them in a pram at the same time. Then I remembered the work: the breast-feeding, the lack of sleep, the constant watching over them, putting on winter clothes for the usual minus ten for several months; bringing and picking them up from Kindergarten; cooking, playing, staying home when they were ill, always one after the other ... years and years of this hard work, which I had forgotten all about because it was such a joy. I had kept them in mind, not thinking about myself. All the work it was, I had forgotten there and then, because I forgot myself and thought about them. This work with children was not a personal satisfaction or an achievement that I could put on my curriculum vitae: '4 million changes of nappies', '600 litres of mother's milk produced per year', etc. No, it was work of a different kind, made in a symbiotic relationship with the small ones; a natural and obvious service to them. All my work for them was nothing to me, just a silent, monotonous, energy-consuming work – but to them it was work that was much more valuable than my professional work in this one, basic sense: it was a pure service.

At that time I had of course never reflected on this work as being a service to God and also to others – it was simply what came with motherhood. But now I could see that this was a service to Him. Work must be well done, but that is just a *necessary*, but not at all *sufficient* condition for it to be a way to God. It is only when it is a service to Him and to others that it acquires a meaning beyond itself. Even in a purely human perspective one sees that work as service is nobler than work as self-fulfilment and self-development. The work as self-fulfilment develops oneself, and that is good. This is a duty to oneself, to use one's talents as well as possible.

But this is only the first step of what work can and should be. I want to manage to do this, I want this professional challenge; I strive to be best in my field – all this is good and should be aimed at. But then, when this is on the right track, it is time to consider to what extent one's work is a service to others. In the service-perspective, I would venture to say that my work as a mother is much more important than my work as a professor or as a politician, although both of these occupations are, or at least should be, full of service.

It is obvious that it is humanely attractive and noble to discover that someone works for others – that a politician works for the common interest of all of society and not only for his or her own advancement; that a doctor really thinks about the best for the patients and not only about his income and status, etc. When one sees that this is the case, it is so surprising and so attractive. At this time when everything in society seems to revolve around the individual and personal advantage, this really stands out. One can hardly believe that anyone would work for anything beyond the sheer self-interest. An American book I came across is even entitled: *Morals: What's in it for me?*

Then there is the pleasure of helping and serving. Serving others: What's in it for me? One could ask. Well, there is the truly joyful feeling of being useful, of being human, of being nobler than your usual self. It does good to do good. Many of us work for ourselves all the time, but when we once in a while actually serve others and help them, we are surprised to learn how satisfying that actually is. It is not strange that rich people turn to philanthropy – it is just too little too late.

Thus one catches glimpses of another reality in those rare moments of serving disinterestedly. The cramp of the self is replaced by self-giving for a moment, and one is in touch with the really human self. It is as if one wakes up to a long-forgotten reality, and one has a insight that this is the key to something fundamental, to an order of things beyond oneself.

Again, in a human context, work as service is gratifying: the nurse who helps the sick knows this; the teacher who helps a weak pupil knows this, but often the mighty in business life are far, far from any human insight in this respect. Work as service is the royal road to improving the world itself – it is in fact the precondition for politics beyond mere power struggle, and it is the key to human sympathy and *communitas*. This work needs to be done well, but then it needs to be directed well, too: as service to others and to society.

In Christian perspective this service is the practical love for others; doing with deeds what charity expects.

The moment one can turn one's work into service, one has made a major step; crossed a large barrier. I love my work for the professional reasons: it is fulfilling, demanding, challenging. I seek work that is just like that: work that will make me stretch for better results, for achieving more, for making me more competent. I detest incompetence. A business leader of the Scandinavian Airline SAS, Hans Dahlgren, said: 'If you think competence is expensive, try a little incompetence', in response to those who complain about high prices for consultants. The consultant's fees may well be too high, but one thing is certain: incompetence is completely worthless and is really an insult to God and His creation.

So competence is also a function of being virtuous in realising that human talents must be developed fully, and also that the devil will always seek to make you content with the mediocre because excellence requires effort. 'Knowledge is painful', my German teacher used to say. He was referring to all the German grammar you must learn by heart in order to speak correctly. There is no other way to acquire competence.

The continous will power needed to conquer yourself in order to stay competent and to carry through a job is thus a training ground for the virtues. It is like training in athletics. But this is not enough; it is rather a necessary preparation for becoming useful in God's plan for you. Then you can start to be useful, to serve. Serving others requires that you have advanced enough in your spiritual life to see that the mission is part and parcel of your relationship with God: He wants you to sanctify the world; nothing less.

How well do you serve others through your work? That does not depend on what kind of job you have. It rather depends on what kind of disposition you have to the work. As a mother I never reflected on the work-as-service that I rendered my children – and still do – but there are women who do not want children because it ties them down and represents too much work.

It is not easy to work as a service. It is much easier to work for oneself. But if one tries to see human work from God's angle for a moment, it is clear that it can only be useful for Him if it improves us, others, and the world itself. And it is equally clear that that work-as-service gives us the same rare joy that self-forgetfulness does. But how can one move from work as self-fulfilment to work as service? It seems like a pious wish; nothing more.

Work as Love: The Third Key

When I thought less about myself and more about my children, I found the third key to the importance of work. The Christian meaning of things is always hidden in everyday life. It is we who are half-blind throughout most of our lives.

After my three years as state secretary, I had returned to normal professional life. The transition had been difficult, but after some months I was settled in a new job which satisfied me and which gave new challenges. I did not miss the old one. But this was all about work as professional challenge, not work as service.

What I had overlooked in my years as a foreign policy maker, was that making appearances and creating policy were not of the first order of importance in God's perspective. They were well and good in themselves – at least most of them time – but what seemed to improve the world to the human eye did not necessarily do so in the divine perspective. I had mistakenly thought that the tangible and visible results of my work was what counted. In the eyes of the world, yes, but what about the supernatural perspective?

Again it was my children who taught me a lesson. I had been away from them so much during those years, and hardly had time for them. I had even written a book about how important motherhood is, meaning every word of it; but I had not really penetrated the matter. Now that I suddenly had time for the children, I realised how much I had neglected them. It was not only a matter of time, it was a matter of being mentally present. They had missed me much more than I had realised because I had been so preoccupied with my important work.

Important in what sense? Modestly important to the world of politics, much more important to me in professional terms; but in terms of service to others, to those entrusted to my care? In God's perspective they come first. I now had time for them again, and this made me see my work in a truer perspective: Coming home at regular hours each day, taking the time to listen to their stories about the day's events, reading and playing with them – all this I realised now, was work that is of capital importance to their human development. They need me most of all, and God has placed them closer to me than anyone else. This silent work is a work of love, and easy to see as such, because one loves one's children. This silent work consists of being at home for the children at regular times, making sure that they have their dinner; helping them with their homework; being there for them. Love is the prime mover of this work, which counts as nothing in the eyes of the world. But in God's perspective this is perfect work: a service done for love. Yes, you have to know how to clean and cook and play to do it well – but in addition you need to love in order to really do this work so that your children are given not only their due, but more.

This example is so simple, and the work involved is also simple. But it is an excellent example nonetheless. The love for one's children is the best way for work to become a service, because most parents have this love. One need not love God so much in order to work selflessly for these small others. But through this love for children one also finds the love for Christ – when I work well for them, I find Christ in the middle of this little family.

In other types of work He can always be found as well, although that may not be so obvious. But if one seeks Him first, one finds the strength to work as a service. The help to do so is given.

'Incarnated' Politics?
An Excursion to Santiago de Compostela

From a bird's-eye view, from the top of the mountains, one sees the city more clearly. This is analogous to the view God has, the supernatural perspective which we can also gradually acquire, at least in glimpses, but always 'through a glass darkly'.

Since my passion is politics, I had given much thought to how a Christian polity should be. I reflected on how to apply the Christian perspective to the earthly city, as a member of the Pontifical Council for Justice and Peace as well as in my capacity as a Christian Democrat. What would an 'incarnated' European polity look like? What would be God's perspective?

In the jubilee year 2000 I was invited to address 50,000 youth on pilgrimage to Santiago de Compostela. Here I had the chance to put the reflections and experience I had made over many years into a speech. This is what I told that large, youthful European audience:

'I read a lead article in Newsweek *magazine with the title 'Is God dead?' It records the speedy decrease of organised Christianity in Europe. Fewer and fewer attend church, fewer and fewer go to confession, and fewer and fewer believe in the authority of churches and tradition. The picture seems bleak indeed. If the 'success' of Christianity is measured by its visible power in our societies, then we have nothing to celebrate. It rather seems that 2000 years have resulted in very little if anything at all: the once so-Christian states have disappeared, giving way to secular pluralism. There are no 'Catholic' states of old left, and the Lutheran state churches in Scandinavia are in the process of changing. The Swedish state church is being dismantled. Knowledge of Christianity is disappearing, and traditional public manifestations of the faith as well.*

Have we lost the battle of Christianising Europe?

I think not. Every age has its political system and its way of defining the status of religion. In our age we have achieved the co-existence of pluralist democracy and religious freedom. True, there are tensions and will be tensions, but we have a clear separation of the spheres of politics and religion and the protection of the religious sphere inscribed in the pre-eminent internationanal human rights instruments.

Europe today is a place for all religions, and also for those who have none. What is essential, is that Christians are free to proclaim and live their religion, free to seek to offer their Christian values in the public sphere and to work so that these values will underlie politics. Not to impose them, to offer them – there will never be any true Christianity unless it is based on acceptance and internalisation.

What I am saying is that without really Christian people it is no good to have Christian structures and Christian traditions. Thus, our concern should be with how Christian we are – as the salt of the earth. Our task is essentially the same as that of the first Christians who worked in an environment where their faith was largely unknown.

Is this good or bad news? That's an irrelevant question. The key is to recognise the situation and to get to work. I don't think the first Christians wasted much time fretting over this question. They acted instead.

Communicating the faith

The first rule of communication is that it is you who fails if the receiving end does not understand your message. When people do not understand what we say, it is we who are at fault – never them. This simple idea has major implications: the Christian message is always and everywhere the same, but it may be communicated in vastly different ways. I rather like scholastic philosophy because I once studied it, but I realise that the arguments of the scholastics would convince no one today. Proofs of the existence of God seem utterly irrelevant to us.

What speaks to modern people is the existential mode. The Pope has understood this perfectly well: his encyclicals are written in a moving, modern language that speaks to the heart as well as to the mind. He tells us of his love for Christ, and of Christ's love for us.

Perhaps the modern way is the 'short cut': we want to hear about causes to live for and die for. Love is that cause, although many do not yet know it. I think very many long for a life of virtues, but again, do not know it. Material satisfaction leaves an emptiness. One looks, somehow, for ideals in life. That ideal of life is found in Christ. I wish we could all be more daring in our way of communicating this – tactful and respectful, yet bold. What we must say, is that this has been our experience. If we are authentic, then the others will at least wonder: What is their secret?

Today in the western world there are many who seek spiritual meaning; indeed, who seek some kind of meaning in their lives. But many of them seek it from a post-modern vantage point: they look for an existential experience that will give them meaning. Often they turn to New Age sects, popular culture, mixing elements of all into their own 'a la carte' religion.

This is indeed an age of complete subjectivism and individual freedom – there are no authorities that seem to have any influence any longer. The same phenomenon is valid for politics: Half the electorate changes parties from election to election, and seem to make their own menu of elements from socialism and liberalism, to give you one example. I often hear of young people who think that it is fine to make their own religious mix: they find elements from eastern religions attractive, as well as some from Christianity. This situation, which frightens many, can perhaps be summed up in the remark an old Benedictine friend of mine made about a younger brother: 'He has no philosophical system – it is all pragmatic.'

My friend was amazed at this, I am not. But all this poses the challenge of communicating the Christian faith in new ways and by new means. This also holds for the public aspects of the faith; those that are directly relevant to politics.

We know that God is not dead, and are therefore not depressed by Newsweek's *headline. But we ought to be very clear about the need for a new way of evangelising. As stated, our situation today is like that of the first Christians who also lived in an environment that was pagan, and where the new faith was met with hostility. So we have little reason to complain – others have done this before us. And the faith has always been introduced in new ways, depending on the circumstances.*

One who has no faith would be depressed by the situation in Europe today – but one who believes will be optimistic that so many have a spiritual quest.

Today people are not impressed by structures and tradition. They seek testimony – personal testimony, personal experience. The example of other Christians is therefore the primary tool for evangelisation. People are curious about why one can believe, in the middle of ordinary life, in modern society, anything as incredible as God making man, and resurrecting man. How can you and I – who are just like the non-believing 'you's and 'I's we meet everywhere – be normal yet actually profess this belief, they ask. And the hope of meaning in life, an afterlife that puts this short life in perspective – how can one believe in that?

We must be inventive in our ways of bringing Christ to others. This requires, like in the first period of Christianity, that we start from a recognition that we cannot assume anything in terms of general knowledge of, and recognition for, Christianity in our societies. People we meet daily may not share any tradition with us; rather, they will shun tradition and the established churches. Further, they will not see the need to put things into any kind of 'system', be it theological, philosophical, or ideological. For instance, when I discuss abortion with friends and colleagues and point out that once abortion is legal, then we cannot say no to euthansia, they usually do not see my point, which is one of logic.

Christianity and politics

Christianity and politics do not have an easy relationship. On the one hand, Christianity shuns politics and should never accept being politicised.

On the other hand, Christianity has everything to do with politics. Christianity is revolutionary in the most radical sense: it calls for a life of self-giving, and the incarnation of Christ in every aspect of life and society.

We all know the ideological development of Catholic social doctrine, and we know that there are Christian Democratic parties in Europe. I myself represent the Norwegian one, as the first Catholic in their history. Further, you are aware of the principles of solidarity and subsidiarity, as well as the construction of Christian Democractic thinking based on the Christian view of the human being. We have an ideology which places us as a third way between, yet distinct from, socialism and liberalism.

All this is well and good, but I want to speak with you in a more direct and practical way. I have talked about the need for *daring apostolate – a personal call for every Christian. Today's Europe is largely secularised, and we cannot assume any famil-iarity with our faith in many places. This gives us a unique challenge. We have to act in the same manner as the first Christians: like them, we cannot assume any knowledge of what it means to be a Christian, neither in public nor in private life.*

But this development towards secularisation, which contin-ues all over Europe, has also meant that the public *character of Christianity has disappeared. Today we notice how Christianity is less and less tolerated in public opinion. That is to say, it is tolerated only when it is a private activity: I collect stamps as a hobby; you 'pursue' your Christian faith. You can go to Mass, you can pray, you can work for the faith within the social sphere of the Church, and you can do social work as a Christian. But if you point out that Christianity is not a private matter, but 'news' that intends to transform both the human being and the world, then you are surely in for trouble.*

Today there is little tolerance in western society of what we usually call missionary work, which in fact is the very essence of the Christian's duty. There is also little tolerance of the fact that religious freedom – as stipulated in international legal norms of human rights, such as the Universal Declaration of Human Rights, explicitly includes the right to missionary work, to public worship, and to parental prerogatives for teaching and educating one's children in one's own religion.

My clear impression is that today the very idea of someone claiming truth value for something – as do all religions – is met with the reaction that the idea of truth itself is intolerant and undemocratic. If something is true, it implies that something else is untrue. Today this seems somehow intolerant: that there can be truth, and that this truth can be discovered. It is far easier to create God in one's own image.

Thus, there is a tremendous tension between western public opinion and Christianity. This should be recognised. I think the 'solution' is to have enough space for religious practise and public expression: Christians claim truth; Muslims claim truth, Jews claim truth, atheists claim truth – and they all co-exist in a pluralist democracy. At a recent seminar on religious freedom someone, an agnostic, said: 'Then all religions must stop claiming truth and find some compromise'. This led to a scream from all the religious people present, and they represented all the religions I mentioned: What an utterly stupid and unrealistic proposal! This chap has not understood that one's religious conviction is far more important than anything else in life.

The 'solution' is that truth claims can live well in democracy. Democracy is not about the ultimate issues in life, such as the meaning of life and the existence of God. It is about a minimal common ground in norms and morals so that problems can be solved and pluralism can blossom. It is also an arena for discussion, and offers an openness that we have never before had in history for debating religious issues. So when I sometimes meet fellow Catholics who are afraid of democracy and pluralism, I am sorry on their behalf.

And there are still states that claim to be democratic where religious freedom is suppressed; and also states where religion is used instrumentally to promote violent conflict and excessive nationalism. Bosnia and Kosovo are in Europe.

But let us not forget that the lack of a common Christian world-view means that notions such as moral theology, sin, and forgiveness have no meaning to the non-believer, and seem to him or her to represent repressive old structures. Likewise, the notion of human dignity of all and the sacredness of human life carry no particular meaning either. The key concepts we use to describe our Christian reality do not reach beyond ourselves anymore. To most, life is the given here and now. It ends in the death of the body, and there is only what you can see and touch – material reality.

This represents new and difficult challenges to us – in terms of communication, explanation, persuasion.

This starting point has profound implications for politics. On the one hand, we claim and we know that Christians must be leaven in society, and that all of society must become imbued with Christ. We want the truth of the human being to be the basis for politics – that the human being is capable of tremendous self-giving and solidarity, that he needs to be free to develop his religious life, that he has a natural ability and desire to form a family, to raise children, and to enrich society through his work. We know that all goes wrong where the state politicises the family and the Church, but that the state must support both institutions. We also know that the solidarity of the Christian extends to the whole human family, as a brotherhood, and that politics must be used to redistibute wealth and to create real welfare states.

We know, in other words, that our Christian mission extends to all of our personal life as well as our lives as citizens. It would be a complete failure if we confined our Christian life to the private sphere. There are many Christians I know who do just that. They say that the persecution they sense in the public sphere is so unpleasant that they prefer to be 'safe' within their own little private world.

They are wrong. How would Christianity have survived in Europe if the first Christians had done the same?

Thus, the goal is very clear: to act as leaven in society, including politics. The starting point for so doing is difficult, because of a steady process of secularisation. However, with this process old sclerotic forms of Christinanity also disappear: clericalism in so-called Catholic states, and the conventional Christianity among all those who are only nominally Christian. I see no reason to regret this, quite the opposite. There can only be real faith or nothing. Christianity is no bourgeouis lifestyle; it is a scandal to most; a fire on the earth.

The Political Issues of Importance

But what specifically is the relevance of Christianity to politics? I would say that there are four areas of special importance: respect for human dignity as an absolute value; support for the family, also in economic terms; respect for the freedom of religion and Churches; and national as well as international solidarity, also across generations.

In these areas Christians should be active: as voters, as citizens, as politicians, as moulders of public opinion. Let me attach a few comments to each of these areas.

Human dignity: Today we see a particularly utilitarian tendency to see others in terms of their usefulness to us. We worship youth, beauty, effectiveness, and achievement in our societies. The old and the sick are sometimes barely tolerated. The unborn are invisible and therefore do not count, and the same goes pretty much for the old and sick. As family ties become less important in society, these people are thought to be the concern of the state rather than of us. It is very easy to rob them of their respect, which is their due as human beings.

We must help society regain respect for the human person. This is the only way to combat abortion and euthanasia, as well as all other inroads made against human dignity in the field of genetic engineering and bioethics.

We must restore the sense of mystery and sacredness about the human person so that people will realise that a person is infinitely more than a heap of flesh and bones. There is a beauty, often hidden, about an old person or a sick person, but only an eye that sees the person beyond the body can discover this. All of us, at one time or another, realise that the other is our Mitmensch – our brother in a very real sense. Yet this ability to recognise all others as fellows must be trained and cultivated, lest it die to us.

I think the Christian in politics must act as a constant reminder of the existential fellowship of all persons, regardless of the circumstances they are in. We must not remain indifferent to our fellows; yet it is very easy to show solidarity only with our kin.

We cannot hope for any new and more fruitful debate on abortion and euthanasia unless we succeed in this. After three decades of abortion on demand in my country I find that most people are completely indifferent to the humanhood of the foetus before three months gestational age. It simply does not exist. Likewise, there is a large and growing indifference to old people – they are marginalised in terms of influence anyway. There are a tremendous number of lonely old people around.

Thus, we must be very aware of the tendency to talk about abortion and euthanasia as the only instances of disrespect for human dignity. We must never confine our concern only to these extreme instances. We are not credible in our defence of human dignity unless we also include a general commitment to solidarity with all, not least in the economic sense.

This brings me to the second issue, solidarity. We do not respect human dignity if we allow for large discrepancies in economic and social welfare. Today market liberalism and its corrollary, consumerism, are the key problems. There is the infamous gap which is widening between poor and rich states, but there is also more and more power vested in market actors to the detriment of political actors. We see this in global capitalism and we see it within each European state.

The labour side has lost bargaining power because capital has become global, and employers increasingly take in or lay off people with the hausse *and the* baisse *of the stocks. There seems to be no* ethos *whatsoever left on the part of the employer – short-time profit and not development that benefits employers and community alike, seems to be the only motive. This in turn makes it almost impossible for an employee to settle down and plan a family.*

In my view capital has far too much power today. We know that the old socialist welfare state did not work, but we must not rescind on the concept of the welfare state. There is a clear need for the state to redistribute in order to attain economic justice within society. For instance, I find it unacceptable that one's parents' income and not hard work and talent should decide whether one can go to university; or that a pregnant woman should be unable to have her child because there is no social allowance. Likewise, there is a clear need to sustain families when they cannot provide enough income through work, or when unemployment happens.

But the picture today in Europe is bleak in this respect: economic differences are widening, and jobs are less secure than before. There has not been a good replacement to socialism in terms of welfare state thinking apart from Catholic social teaching. We need to put that teaching into practice.

Internationally, donor fatigue is rising. Fewer and fewer give less and less development aid. In addition, the values of materialism dominate us. It is indeed hard for a mother like me to fight the influence of the market on my children.

Christians must live solidarity in all aspects of life. Wealth creation must not be for oneself and one's family only, but for the whole human community. Further, wealth is only a means, not an end, like all material possessions.

This is a hard lesson to practise. Most of us are very interested in material comfort and ownership. It gives an easy life and it gives status. We all desire this or that, and have to fight this dominant tendency all the time. For non-Christians it is even more difficult to realise that things are but a means to something else.

Today there is tremendous power in the market, and concomitantly less power in politics. We must fight to regain political power because the political is about the ordering of all of society, to which economics must be subordinate. With globalisation, this is much more difficult than in the era of the nation-state.

But power comes to politics if and when we put our energy into it, disregarding our own private concerns about wealth. We can and must invest power in political institutions again – through your participation, and mine.

Christians must share in all senses, also the economic one. There is no mistake about the preference Christ had for the poor. Indeed, he was also one of them.

The third area which is important in politics is the family. Today there are several challenges to the health of the family: unemployment and job insecurity for young people who are about to start a family; less political support for families and thus a weaker position for this institution, and a massive increase in divorces as well as individualism. It is no longer a foregone conclusion that one will marry and have a family, and the very concept of the family is itself being challenged.

We record that birth rates in Europe are very low, especially in Spain and Italy, but also in Eastern Europe. I like to boast that Norway has the highest birth rate in Europe, and this is due to good social policies like a one-year paid maternity leave, paternity leave and job security for the mother when she returns to employment. The politicians in Europe must realise that today women are as well or even better educated than men, and that they consequently both want to work and – usually – have to work for economic reasons.

The old sex role pattern has definitely changed with the educational revolution. If women lose their jobs when they have children, they are not going to have children. Today this is *often the case, and this angers me very much: How can politicians complain that women have so few children if they do nothing to ensure that women can combine motherhood and work? If Europe's women had real equality with men in the sense that having children would not endanger their professional careers, we would see a different birth rate. I am so happy that finally women will be able to influence politics and professional life, but this should not be at the expense of having children.*

In order to make it possible for the family to survive in Europe, we must have strong social and economic policies that protect it. Fathers must take their rightful share in housework and responsibility for the family. Isn't it good that finally fathers will spend time raising children on a par with the mother instead of being away at work? I am convinced that we can find work-sharing schemes that allow parents more time with children – like my government has done in Norway.

But this is of great urgency in European politics – already there is far too low a birth rate to sustain the population, to mention but one important aspect. My message is that women refuse to continue to do double work – outside and inside the home, and they also refuse to endanger their jobs when they get pregnant. Does an employer ask a man how many children he has or whether he will have any? Does an employer ask a woman such questions?

Yes, he does, regardless of whether it is legal or not.

This is also an age of tremendous individualism and little faith in the ability to stay married for a lifetime. Most people seem to want to try out marriage or at least cohabitation to see if it works, but not make any firm commitment. It is very easy to walk out, and this is fully accepted by society's norms today. Christians have a big challenge in trying to show the point of lifelong marriage. To most the idea sounds like a nightmare: to spend perhaps forty or fifty years with the same man or woman, losing one's precious freedom. How can anyone dare to make such vows? Why would anyone want to, anyway? Better to play it safe and retain the exit option.

A Norwegian author who has much inspired me, Sigrid Undset, wrote as far back as in the 1920s that lenient marriage laws acted like a door that was always open, letting a constant draft into the home. The temptation to leave was always there, presenting itself as perfectly acceptable. Today this draft is like a gale force wind: almost no one speaks for lifelong marriage in public. True, it is easy to admit that stable marriage is good for both children and society, but will that argument convince the individualist of today? After all, marriages that last seem, as far as I can see, to be the exception rather than the rule. And we all know that in the old days there were many marriages that must have been awful and that would have ended in divorces if that option had been a viable one.

So what speaks for lifelong marriage? As Christians we know that life is ultimately about serving, and that love is also ultimately about self-giving. I think this truth is what we have to communicate to others, primarily by our own example. Those couples who leave each other when it storms, will usually experience that the same will happen to them again: there will be another storm in a new relationship, and in the end they realise that the grass was not greener on the other side after all.

It is of course not easy to find out that love is not primarily about self-satisfaction, but about self-giving. Our children teach us that, but also in a marriage one must accept this, and then gradually realise that it is true. In a Christian perspective this is much easier, because in Christ we find outpouring love, a total self-giving. We also realise that suffering has a meaning and that we can leave all our pain in His hands. In a secular context, all this sounds like nonsense.

But there is one way of communicating these truths: through your own example. You can show others that it is possible to undertake the commitment of lifelong marriage and that it is possible to accept and sometimes even to solve problems. Moreover, you can show others that there is a mature happiness that results from these battles fought: the serenity of someone who masters himself and who stands by commitments. Many times this will only become apparent with time, but I think it essential to simply be different in our society. When divorce is regarded as normal and commonsensical, as it is today, we need to show what the institution of marriage and family really is. It is not an old-fashioned repressive bourgeois *institution, but a safe haven for the human being, especially for the children.*

Children suffer tremendously in divorces – most people are willing to admit that. Then the next step is to convince them that their children are the foremost reason for their marriage to last, and that marriage and family is hard, practical work – not an institution based on feelings.

In a political perspective, we know that stable families are absolutely key to the survival of society: who will raise your children unless you do it? In my view, the most pressing political task in Europe is to redress the imbalances regarding the family: states should not have a 'value neutral' view of this, but say clearly that marriage is preferable to cohabitation, and that divorces are sad tragedies rather than normal practice. Once this is spelt out, states should support their views in economic terms. There are relatively few politicians who dare to be clear about this today because it is more politically correct to say that 'lifestyle' issues are private concerns. This may very well be; but what is a public *issue are the conditions for raising children. Hence the public importance of the stable family.*

My fourth issue in politics is non-interference. This may seem a really non-political issue, and perhaps it once was. Now, however, we have to restate the definitions of human rights instruments that define the freedom of religion and make sure that there remain non-political spheres in society. Freedom of religion means that church teaching sometimes conflicts with public opinion and majority views in democracy. The right to deviate from public opinion must be ensured in practice, as it is in theory. Otherwise, majority views turn into majority tyranny.

Likewise, we must remind ourselves that there are non-political spheres of life and of society. This includes civil society, family, and churches. The temptation to politicise these spheres is always there. I regard this as a key area where Christians must act.

Unless Christianity is a living reality to people, there is no point in seeking to make it influential in politics. There will be no support or even acceptance for this, and political structures that are nominally Christian will become sclerotic; a dead weight. Thus, the work of Christians to bring the faith to others must go hand in hand with their work in politics.

The Norwegian Christian Democratic party, which I repre-sented in government, started as an outgrowth of the lay man's movement. Its aim was to act as leaven in society. Its founders were very insistent that the politicians in the party be Christians themselves.

I think they were right. Naturally it is important to have a clear programme and a clear ideology, and to be able to argue in truly political terms in political forums – but the key element in all this work is that of the salt, to use the parable. It is fully possible to act professionally in politics and at the same time seek to be oneself as a Christian in public. In Norway, at least half of the cabinet are Christians. In my ministry, the Foreign Office, those who are Christian start the day with prayer together. The prime minister, a Lutheran pastor, never conceals his Christianity, and is in fact one of the most popular prime ministers ever in Norway. People notice his professionalism; but more than that, they notice his integrity. The same can be said for other ministers. My point is not to boast, but simply to say that we must be ourselves, as Christians, fully, openly; and of course also ourselves in our professional capacity. We can only lead lives that are marked by unity – if not, it all becomes false.

There is no point in preaching Christian values in politics unless we also make people receptive to Christianity. Let us therefore be less concerned with political labels, structures and conventions, and feel free to find new ways of communicating the good news. The harvest is big; but all we have to do is what we can.
But we have to do that.'

All these ideas need to be put into practice. They are a blueprint, as I see it, for a society imbued with Christianity. But all 'integrisme' is doomed to fail. It is the people themselves, individually, who have really to *be* Christian. Withour *being*, there can be no sustainable *action*.

CHAPTER 7

THE HIDDEN LOVE

In the treatment of mental patients pscychiatrists some-times had to employ the straitjacket. It is a jacket where the arms are tied around the body, so that the patient cannot harm others or himself. It is also a term we use when we feel imprisoned, unfree.

Many times life seems like a straitjacket. You have to go to work; that job you dislike; you have to earn the money for your family; you are perhaps in a 'hopeless' marriage, you are dissatisfied with the parameters of your life, and long for a change, for freedom. Today most people don't stay in such situations for the sake of duty, but when they break up and change spouse and job, they often find them-selves in another and similar straitjacket. After a while this one seems even worse than the first, because now one knows that there is no real escape by jumping the fence: the straitjacket is *inside* you; a terrible discovery indeed.

Restlessness, boredom, fear, meaninglessness. Amidst money, power, status, things, diversions, pleasures. Never have so many in the western world been able to get all these things. The narcissism is complete: I am able to buy happiness, or at least, satisfaction. But never have so many been so unhappy. We are simply not happy human beings anymore. Spontaneity, joy – where is it?

You know joy from your own childhood: the day you all went on a special vacation, or when you came home with poor grades and your mother comforted you. When there was a little extra for the family after hard work; when money was scarce but the joy of that special effort and the love from your parents created such a peace and happiness in you. You did not have all the things we have now, but you had more time and no one was allowed to think solely of himself. Work then seemed so naturally meaningful: to serve a family that depended on it. Perhaps because we were poor – at least in Norway – there was more virtue and more service.

Looking back, you know that it was not the money or the things that really made you happy, although as a child you thought so when you finally got the toy you had wanted so badly. No, it was the love of those who cared for you, their selfless service to their children that created this deep happiness in you. This you only understood much later, as an adult.

I am not nostalgic, and do not want those times of poverty back. But today we think that we do not need each other any longer. We want to have the freedom to pursue ourselves all the time: diets, clothes, things, whatever is in the market place. When there is a situation, rarely, of serving and helping others, we are stunned at ourselves; that we are able to help, and more so, that we are so happy when we do it. What kind of hidden dimension of life is this?

I work in business circles and in political circles, in areas where people are sophisticated and calculating. Often the tone is tough: rough jokes, sarcastic remarks. The persons I meet play these roles, perhaps I do, too. It is not so easy to be different. But how much loneliness and unhappiness is behind the successful façades? The poverty today is human and spiritual. How can one reach out? Break that shell?

Go away and have another experience. The humbug of the market now also includes 'lifestyles' – take a course and become a 'whole' person. Design your spiritual self, add a little something from each religion. Get warm inside, feel good about yourself. Take your pick in philosophy.

All this is mixed and sold to the poor persons of today

who have no knowledge of human nature, of the European tradition of *askesis*. They should read the 'Confessions' by St Augustine, more thrilling suspense than any crime story.

Christ is the only answer to the unhappiness of the human heart, to the boredom, restlessless and impatience. The cure is not somewhere else, because life's parameters are not there by chance; they are part of a plan. This is tremendous news: part of a plan, made by someone who knows you. In fact, *designed* just for you, one of billions of human beings in history.

This is so amazing that it cannot be fully grasped.

And we do not need to grasp it either. But we do need to try. The ascetic programme of the Stoics is appealing as self-defence in a hostile world, but it can never make for happiness. Happiness – or rather, joy – is the deep peace and love inside that comes from a source. That source is within you, but it is God himself. When you earnestly seek Him, you also find Him. This is the secret: you have to be deadly honest, not calculating. You cannot cheat and say. 'Ok, if you exist, I'll take you into account'. No, you must desire Him so much that you pursue Him, although in the beginning you do not know this and seem to simply 'stumble' across Him. But once you are aware that He is, then you must go after Him. If you happen to have some kind of crisis in your life, that is usually a great help on the way because it makes you humble.

Then surprises come your way. On the bus, when you are suddenly full of joy because you remember Christ. It is He who watches over you, and He lets you know His presence when you need some consolation. Perhaps there are long periods of restlessness and boredom. You go to Mass and are distracted, you continue the daily routines and feel like a machine, and you want to abandon this pursuit of Christ. Then again, when you least expect Him, He is there and makes you wildly happy. You say to Him: 'I love You so much, I love You!', and the word love cannot capture your joy, which is unlike anything you have ever known.

Then you stray again, you make detours, you are back to

your dry life, and you strive with your daily tasks, trying to pray and to live virtuously. You fail, but you do not abandon your life's project, because deep inside you know that He is alive and that He is God.

The joy you have known is pure love, and you cannot leave Him for good. Even if you do, you will always long for that love which you have tasted, which transforms you and your work, giving life the only meaning there is. This love spurs you on and on, and you thirst for it, search for it, long for it. This is the truth of human life, the pearl hidden in the field, as Scripture says.

Once you have tasted this love, you will never be happy without it.

The happiness we search is to be loved unconditionally

This book is a different love story. It is about discovering what love is, something which is not quick and easy. It takes a long time to learn how God loves the human being, and how we should love each other. Even when one knows this, it is very difficult to practise such love. It is only possible, I think, when one loves Christ so much that one realises that one must love all His creatures because one loves Him. The love for others in a way goes 'through' Him. Without Him, I cannot see how one can love one's enemies and even those that we find unattractive and uninteresting; even downright vulgar and disgusting. The natural propensity for all of us is to shy away from all those we do not like, and we easily look with condescension on others. But with Him, we are gradually enabled to see Him in others. Then we also love them, for His sake.

How can be discover what love is? How can we practise it?

I think it is written somewhere in the Book of Psalms that 'You lured me after you; I could not resist'; something like that. It is the language of passion, longing and deep love that we find in the Bible.

I met a Swedish convert, and asked her why she converted. 'I simply fell in love', she said. 'It would never have happened otherwise. That love drew me to the Church.' My experience was the same: falling in love, then learning, slowly, what love is. And St Augustine, like so many others later, was imbued with this love once he discovered it. In his famous *Confessions* he wrote, with great sorrow: 'Too late did I love Thee'.

God is love. This sounds like a cliché, often expressed by enthusiastic young believers, written on walls, like a hippie slogan. But what does it mean, really? One cannot dissect and deduce about love; it is ridiculous. But there are at least two momentous questions: Is God's love the real love, and how is it related to human love as we know it? And if this is so, how do we discover and practise this love?

Christ always asked for love. 'Do you love me?' He asked Peter; not 'do you have the competence and leadership ability to steer my Church?' He simply asked whether Peter loved him, three times to absolve him of his threefold denial when Christ was taken to Pilate. In terms of competence, Peter had none other than fishing. He would be the least suitable candidate for a top management position, as the leadership of a new organisation in a hostile milieu certainly was. But all that was irrelevant: the only requirement was about love.

The ultimate amazement is when one discovers that God died for each one of us, out of His love for us. This is so breathtaking that it cannot be grasped by the limited human mind, but we realise, in a gradual manner, that it is true. We hear it, we read it, but it means nothing to us in the beginning of our Christian life. Then we understand it in proportion to our own ability to love selflessly; in fact, it is this realisation that makes us able to love selflessly.

Christianity is not a set of moral rules or a philosophical system. It is a relationship with a person. This is the essence. The encounter with Christ can be a sudden shock or a gradual discovery. But it is Him we seek in the Mass and in prayer, in conversation and thought. We want to be loved; this is our deep existential longing, and we find this truest of love in God, through His son who was made man. This is the secret, the hidden love, the pearl in the field.

The little boy in the mental hospital in Kosovo who had embraced me: He expressed this deep need and desire to be loved, to be held and caressed. He wanted, above all other needs he had, to be loved. I often think back to that moving moment: I, a complete foreigner, who entered there after bedtime. He, a little boy with nothing in the world. He just abandoned himself to me, demanding to be loved. Nothing before or later has moved me so deeply.

We are like that little boy, deep down, when we are honest with ourselves. The restless quest for meaning, for *raison d'etre*, for fulfilment is a quest for love. This love is also finding who one is and what one's vocation is. It is in a way coming 'home' to what we are destined to be.

The great mystics of the Church have written a lot about this process of abandonment to the loving Father God. These stories are sublime love stories, but they are personal stories. Each person has his own way. Therefore they cannot be read like 'recipes'; like I had once done.

Like a child

It is easy for the children. They abandon themselves to the parents, having blind trust in them and their guidance. For us grown-ups, it often takes a crisis or many. It also takes insistence and prayer.

As I discovered that Christianity is about getting to know God through Christ, His Son made man, I also discovered that I had to gradually forget about my own ego; in fact, try to starve it to death, in order for God to find room. This is only possible becaues one is 'lured' out through falling in love and loving in a more mature way.

We must become humble like children. But how? We who are so important.

God the Father, I His child. Sounds childish? No, it is

serious business, the most serious there is. The divine filiation is the best news around. It means that God is the
Father who watches over you, who holds you in the palm
of His hand. I often felt so alone and abandoned, so lonely
in a naked and meaningless universe. The divine filiation
is God's outpouring love for us, in the here and now, in
every instant. It is not a feeling, although we feel it from
time to time, and are duly grateful for that; but it is an
ontological reality: As the scholastics said in their meta-
physical treatises, we are, exist, insofar as we are like God.

And to be like God is to know how to love.

I often thought about this theoretically, but only in later
years did I experience this: that I am to the extent that I am
fully my potentiality, my vocation, what I am meant to be.
That is something we know immediately when we do
right, do good, act in God's will. The times when we are
really deeply 'in tune' with our best qualities, we are on
the right way, and we know it.

God does the teaching and the guidance on the path of
love. We are drawn by the hidden love we have caught
some kind of glimpse of, while he educates us when we
are able to learn. This requires a purification, an ability on
the part of our soul, which is not there immediately. I saw
it only afterwards, this process of purification, where the
human being is formed 'like the clay in the potter's hand'.

This lifelong process hurts, but it is the necessary condition for being able to, once, love like God loves. The
mystics have many metaphors for this; they talk about
God the sculptor who chisels His work more and more
finely. The chiselling hurts, but is necessary. The sins we
commit daily are not only the 'big' ones which we notice,
but the many small ones that damage like drops falling on
a stone, year after year, finally eroding it. Important,
deadly, but hardly noticeable.

The love of God, which we crave, cannot be fully found
until we are ready.

I will not talk about sins or purification in the abstract,
as it makes no sense. Neither will I talk about it in a
personal sense, as that is my private matter. But it is true

that one sees this only afterwards – how God has allowed temptations and pruned one's selfishness away, at least to some extent. While it lasts, one does not know what is going on, or why. One only knows that it hurts, that is is beyond one's own control, and that one simply has to rely on God. The stubborn and spiritually lazy, like myself, probably need a good dose of this cure.

Eventually, perhaps after many years of having a 'thorn in the flesh', to use St Paul's words, one sees it in perspective and realises that one has passed through a spiritual education. Only afterwards can one understand that this had a meaning and that it was necessary. And then one has come one step closer to God, a new 'conversion' has taken place. One is more in Him than before, and the sign of this is that one is able to love a little more selflessly than before.

One has made one more step on the way. The way is still hidden, but now one knows this, and accepts it more and more. There are probably many more steps on that way, more conversions.

Easter 2001

In Oslo there were ice-cold winds and almost zero degrees. The streets were deserted. It was 13 April, 2001 – 'Good Friday'. Easter in Norway means that everyone takes off to the mountains to ski, or to the Costa del Sol in more recent years. 'Only stray dogs and Catholics are in town', the saying goes. That is because the poor Catholics must go to church, and there are few if any Catholic churches outside the major towns. Like the stray dogs, we presumably have no choice.

This Easter was colder than I can remember of any other. 'The wind are easterly, from Siberia', my father says. If anyone knows about winds, it is he, having lived a long life on the coast. We bravely walk, meeting another Catholic, a Dominican nun. She looks like Batman in the wind.

I do not at all mind the deserted streets and the cold. It

is bland and lonely compared to any Easter in Rome or a Mediterranean city. Here it is truly deserted: everything is closed and no one is around anywhere. It is quiet like the grave, as we say; but that forces one to concentrate on the Easter message.

Without distractions and temptations, it is easier to really think about Christ and meditate on His Passion, the ultimate expression of love. He suffered the most painful and humiliating treatment of all men, yet no one seems to care about Him any more. This year this strikes me more than in previous years: the complete *indifference* of secular society around me.

Christ – only an old history, nothing of interest. Easter here is all about skiing and getting a sun tan in the mountains, or about preparing the boat and putting her to sea. It is a vacation to prepare for spring and summer, and has no spiritual meaning any more.

The Passion seems a complete outrage in such a setting: That God would sacrifice His son to atone for the sins of people who could not care less. This total indifference to Christianity is worse than opposition, I think. In Jerusalem they were agitated, excited, and full of hatred.

Here they are indifferent.

On Palm Sunday the whole family had hurried to church. We met a neighbour who said: 'Where are you off to so early?' 'It is Palm Sunday, we must not be late', I replied. 'Are there still people who take these things seriously?' he remarked. 'Yes, indeed there are', I said. He looked a bit embarrassed. I was clearly some kind of fanatic.

Condescension and ridicule of Christianity is not uncommon in Norway, however. In 1931 a very brilliant author, Arnulf Øverland, made an eloquent but very blasphemous speech about Easter, mocking the Passion and Resurrection. At that time he caused an outrage and was charged with blasphemy. Today that concept is unknown, and no one would raise an eyebrow at any kind of mockery. The population is indifferent to the Easter message; few go to church, and Christians are looked

upon with disdain and suspected of being fundamental-
ists and fanatics.

But this reality around us – in most of western society,
but much more up here than in southern Europe where
Christianity and the Catholic Church are known and at
least still nominally respected – this reality in fact makes it
easier to be united with Christ. One immediately realises
that we suffer like He did, but that none of that can in any
way be comparable to His suffering. One also realises that
He was rejected then, just as He is rejected now. But most
of all one realises that it is a choice for or against Him all
the time, and if you choose Him you can rest assured that
nothing in your surroundings will make it any easier for
you. Thus, you are making the choice against all the
advantages of going with the stream.

You go against the current: but that is proof that you are
really choosing Him for His own sake. You have to be
detached and abandoned to do this, otherwise you will be
worried about human respect and the consequences of
publicly following this madman from Galilee. But there is
more than this logical argument; it goes much deeper. St
Paul says that: 'When I am weak, I am strong.' This
paradox is really and deeply true: only when there is no
'support structure' at all for us, are we able to rely on and
abandon ourselves to God. But we do not choose Him
because it is logical or popular. We choose Him because
we love Him, deep down, perhaps even without realising
it ourselves. We come back to Him, almost reluctantly,
each time we have strayed. We long for Him – nothing
less.

Support and 'success' mean that we do not 'need' God;
or at least, find it hard to rely on Him. It took me so many
years to realise that Christ is present all the time and that
I need Him all the time, not only when I 'get lost' and
realise that I miss Him. I used to promise myself to lead a
steady spiritual life, frequent Mass and prayer, some
meditation during the day at a set time, and trying to keep
a presence of God. This promise was made over and over
and over again, and I never seemed to be able to carry it

through. The result is always the same: one quickly depletes the few spiritual resources that one has, and becomes dissatisfied, superficial, 'forgets' Christ. Then the way back is open, and one has to make it again and again, to restore what was lost. But I was really incredibly slow to learn that I needed 'nourishment' on a regular basis, and that the 'conversation' with God was the most necessary part of my everyday life.

My friend from Copenhagen once wrote to me: 'I love the world and all the hectic activity of work life as long as my heart is always in touch with my Father.' At the time I thought this was a somewhat pious and poetic remark, and did not give it much thought. Only several years later did I really understand what he had meant, and saw that it was a realistic statement of the first importance. He meant that only when he was in contact with God, through loving Him, could he work and love the world effectively. The implication of this was of course that if the loving 'conversation' and relationship between him and His Father God was not there, then he, too, was lost in a worldly life, and would be miserable. I had missed this link – it was the umbilical cord that I had cut off – and still I wondered why I could not be more Christian, why I did not come closer to Christ. I learnt from my own many mistakes that I must keep the contact with my Father intact, otherwise nothing would work in life. Meaning is only possible when the transcendent and divine voice can act and speak. We have to be open and to correspond. I knew it, but I did not follow the simple spiritual advice that I always got: Mass, confession, daily prayer. I prayed only when I felt like it, and that was of course at the times when there was a presence of God during my day.

All the days when I had no 'need' of God and moved entirely on the superficial, material plane of things, I 'forgot' about praying. I was too lazy and disinterested. It is like saying to someone, 'I love you, but only on my conditions and when I feel like it. I'll call you, don't call me.'

The difference between the Christ-man relationship and

human relationships is of course that He calls you again and again, however much you reject Him and forget Him. This is something absolutely amazing which is hidden. You only realise it slowly, after knowing Him for some time. During the first years of my Christian life I had no understanding of the Passion. What was the point? It was a horrible story, but why did it have to happen?

Only much later I saw that it was a *love story*: God loves us to the point of sacrificing His own Son, who suffered more at our hands than any other human being can suffer. We were the protagonists who made Him suffer, and He also atoned for our cumulative sins. This is a mystery, and I do not understand all of it, but I think that the most moving realisation is that Christ loved unconditionally, serving us. There was a total outpouring of self, a total self-giving for mankind. Each time we think we suffer, there is the possibility of seeing that He always suffered more, and that all suffering has a meaning if we want it to. We offer it to Him, and then it becomes true, as is written, 'my burden is light'. Suffering borne with love, for love, become imbued with meaning.

This tremendous love cannot be grasped easily; and one must come close to Christ to know it. But it is easy, not difficult, if one has an open mind. The indifference today is the closed door. Fatherhood implies childhood, and there is the key. Modern secular man thinks he or she is sophisticated and enlightened, when in fact one is full of prejudice. The Christians, they think, are a bit naive and backward to believe. Then one has a 'hard' heart, as it so eloquently is written in Scripture, a heart full of prejudice and cynicism. The way to the Father is through being the children we are.

A child makes mistakes over and over again, falls and hurts himself, and then runs back to the father and mother for help. The child is dependent, is open to impressions, and the child is ready to start over again after falls. The child disobeys, but ultimately admits mistakes. It strikes me that this is how we are before God the Father, and this is exactly how we should be. Childlike behaviour is much better than indifferent, distanced, cynical behaviour.

But it makes no sense to be childlike unless you have a father to relate to.

Friendship with Christ is the way to God. It is a love relationship. It requires attention and constancy on our part, because otherwise we go dry and superficial, living in our own shell of self-centredness again. The difference between this relationship and human relationships is vast, marked by the fact that Christ is always there for us, while we are often not there for Him. My friend had often said. 'Talk with Him. Tell Him you love Him.' In earlier years I had thought that he was overdoing it quite a bit; maybe that his English was a bit simple so that he didn't quite know what he was saying. Christ was then, for me, still a distant refuge that I turned to once in a while, especially when I could not find solutions to problems on my own. But talking with Him daily? Like a friend? Sounded strange to me.

In my own long task of depleting all my spiritual support again and again, of 'running into the wall', of making the same mistake of 'forgetting' about God, I finally came to the conclusion that my friend was realistic. I needed to cultivate my conversation with Christ – what we call prayer – as the condition for living an everyday Christian life. And I needed to do that at exactly those times when I did not feel like it, when I effectively 'forgot' Christ and did not feel any kind of inspiration and presence. I needed prayer and the sacraments like I needed food and water.

This seems incredible to a modern human being who sees the world and the human being in material, empirical terms. Yes, food and water of course, otherwise we die. But non-material, spiritual nourishment? Do we need that? As long as we see life materially, as having no spiritual reality to it, we naturally do not. But the 'proof' of this need lies in the dryness and emptiness we experience when we go without the spiritual nourishment for some days or weeks.

Once you have known a little about seeing life

differently, from a supranatural perspective, you never get peace by being earthbound again. You long for that which you have caught but a glimpse of, but you may nonetheless continue your earthbound life. Human nature, I have gradually and painfully learnt, is not to be trusted very much. One makes resolutions to do what is good for oneself, especially at the moment when one realises that this is the real reality and that one needs the sacraments and the prayer so much, but then we forget, again and again. Therefore the Mass duty on Sundays is the wisest invention, given the way we are. Most non-Catholics I know think this is a repressive and authoritarian practice, imposed on us poor Catholics. 'Isn't it awful to have to go Mass?' a friend asked. 'Well, I would probably never go now unless it had been imposed on me', I said, 'I would have dropped it each time I did not feel like it, and then I would have dropped the Church eventually.' That was a real danger for me for several years. It took me a long time to learn how human nature is, and how it betrays us again and again if we let it. We should not trust ourselves too much, but that is a thought completely alien to modern man.

Catholicism is eminently *realistic*, both about our nature and about the practical ways to stay faithful to Christ. The sacraments are given by Christ as everyday, practical means to retain and improve in the life in Christ. One cannot get by for long without them. Laziness, sensuality, materialism, self-centredness – it all strikes hard unless you keep vigilant. This insight is however extremely hard to come by. As I said, it took me many years. I treated my need for the sacraments and for prayer in a completely cavalier fashion. Each time I 'advanced' in my own self-knowledge was when I had some crisis, 'running into the wall', as I call it.

This was more childish behaviour than childlike behaviour, but eventually I saw how hopeless it was to rely on myself and my whims. Then I also realised that all I could be and indeed am – in front of the Father God, is a child: disobedient, clumsy, dependent, yet capable of loving.

The Father-Child relationship is indeed the right one. Our difficulty is becoming like a child.

Excursion: Getting to know Mary

The one human being who really loved like Christ, perfectly, was Mary. I eventually have come to understand this, but getting to know and accept Mary for me was a long-drawn-out task. That she was able to accept and love the will of God unconditionally is what is great, what makes her the strongest woman in history. But my prejudices were many, so I did not learn about how she loved God until I had cast them off.

One of the major obstacles many converts face in the Catholic faith is Mary. She seems to be outside of any possible reach. Mary, the Mother of God, was deleted from Protestant Christianity with the Reformation, and never made it back until more recent times. Mary is also surrounded by a lot of prejudice, as are the saints. We converts do not like this either; we feel distinctly ill at ease with popular Catholicism, and harbour great suspicion regarding places of pilgrimage and popular *fiestas* in Latin countries.

I had however had one strange experience that could not be explained 'naturally', but which has stayed with me ever since as a beautiful, surprising event. It happened in Annecy in 1993. The whole family, six in all, were on summer vacation. Bathing in the Lac d'Annecy one afternoon, we were surprised by a sudden, strong tempest. We were trapped by the lakeside, standing under a roof in the torrential rain and thunder. We could not move through the park because of the lightning, and the small children started to feel very cold and cry. We waited for about two hours, getting more cold and more wet; the children really in a bad shape. I was getting desperate on account of the children, and no one was in sight in this by now deserted place. Of course no one would dare to walk through the park towards the lake with the danger of lightning striking the trees!

Then, when we saw no way out, and the tempest was becoming stronger, a man suddenly emerged from under the trees. He walked straight towards us and said that he would help us home. He led us, without a word, through the park, and into his modest car. The only thing he said all this time was an apology about the car being too small. He let us out at our hotel and did not heed our desire to invite him in; he just took off as quickly as he had come.

He had a delicate modesty and mysteriousness about him. My husband jokingly said that it was a guardian angel. He just came, helped us, and disappeared. To this day I remember him as someone who came specifically for us.

I recall that it was the feast of SS. Peter and Paul.

But in general I did not believe in 'interventions' and least of all in the extraordinary actions of that kind. It made me feel uncomfortable. Christ was enough; there was no need for more people in my spiritual life. It was hard enough to concentrate on Him.

While it took many years before I realised that I needed daily spiritual routines in order not to jump from crisis to crisis, it took me even longer to become acquainted with Mary and the saints. I had had a rosary in my handbag for all those years, but had never been able to use it. I still find it very difficult, and do not use it often. But I have started to get to know Mary.

Mary: I associated her with the sweet-smiling madonna that all the pious Catholic women prayed to. She was, it seemed, invented for them, fulfilling their need for a feminine role model. Mary was for the women of old, not for me. Only much later have I discovered that Mary is the strongest of women in her unconditional obedience to God's will, in her silent strength when her Son was mutilated and executed, and in her many years with Him as His mother when she knew who He was, but no one else did. But this insight was long in coming, barred by deep-seated prejudices that I share with many.

Then there was all the supersititon, I secretly thought. All those places of apparitions and miracles. I did not believe in any of that of course, and it was true that one did not have to believe in that in order to be a Catholic. My sister-in-law went to Lourdes on pilgrimages, bringing back water that was supposed to heal sickness. I took no interest, and frankly found it a bit appalling. It was completely foreign to me.

For many years I harboured much prejudice about this, although I did not admit that to myself. But Mary was a problem because I realised, intellectually, that she was so important, and I saw how many decent and intelligent people had a close relationship with her. Some people I knew even prayed the rosary every day. Well, they were probably brought up to do so, I thought, as they do in so-called Catholic countries. I once told one of them, 'I do not know Mary at all'. 'Tell her that', she simply said as if she talked about a conversation with her own mother. I tried, not very hard, to pray the rosary, but it never worked. Trying to say the prayers and also meditating on a mystery was too much for me. I still cannot do it properly. But I pray it, in my own strange way, from time to time, on the bus.

So getting to know Mary was not so easy after all, especially as I took little interest. On the contrary, I was a bit concerned about the obvious devotion of the Pope to Mary. Why, I wondered. Because he is Polish, I reasoned. But this redundant explanation was plainly stupid: he is also a towering intellectual who had no need for 'simple' devotions. Likewise, did my friend pray the rosary out of old habits from childhood? Hardly.

So the question of Mary was left unresolved.

Then I happened, by chance, I assumed, to visit places of pilgrimage: First it was a conference in Santiago de Compostela with the EU Commission, then a visit to Fatima in another EU context, and finally, in May 2001, three occasions in a row: Fatima, Santiago de Compostela, and Lourdes, all because of meetings I had to go to for some reason or other.

The first time in Santiago we saw the magificent basilica and were guided to the apostle St James, whose coffin and statue is placed behind the altar. The northern Europeans were a bit embarrassed at seeing people going to confession right there on the floor, in all visibility. The guide assumed we were pilgrims, and channelled us into a row, declaring in a heavy Spanish accent: 'you may now kiss the foot of the apostle'. The incredulous Swedes in the group were utterly shocked, but since I was the only Scandinavian Catholic among us, I took the lead. They all followed suit. But it was foreign not only to them, but also to me.

Some years later we visited, the whole family; this time I was less incredulous, but still with the reserve that comes from deep prejudice. But seeing the true devotion of the many pilgrims made a deep impression. They were genuine in their fervour and adoration. They really were pilgrims, but I was not. I was just a tourist there. It made me uncomfortable. Why was it so hard to accept that such places had a real meaning?

Our children were there. They acted as the natural sceptics children always are, asking how St James came to Compostela, whether he was really in the coffin, and so on. In the crypt under the basilica they were impressed by the excavated bodies from the first centuries after Christ. This was tangible 'evidence'. The children were satisfied in their curiousity, Sophie the youngest even noticing that one of the corpses had bad teeth. 'He did not go to dentist at all', she concluded, 'but I have to.'

But their inquistiveness made me reflect: why must we have our kind of 'proof' all the time? We will not believe unless we have proof. But all those pilgrims throughout the centuries: they believed and they atoned for their sins. That is all that is necessary. Does it really matter whether St James was there?

Bullet-proof

The first time I visited Fatima was in connection with another congress. For the first time I saw someone walking on his knees to do penance. I was so uninformed that I thought the man was crippled, and when he suddenly stood up, I was shocked. Was this a miracle unfolding before my eyes? Then when scores of others came to the chapel on their knees, I understood how stupid I was. But I had no sympathy for what I saw. It seemed superstitious, overdone, strange.

Later I have realised that my prejudices stood in the way of tolerance. All that is asked is that we allow others to worship in their way. They do not impose on us. Why do we impose our views on them? This intolerance of mine was the same attitude that I had had towards the Lutherans in my home town many years back: they were simple and unsophisticated, and I judged them. Likewise, the popular expressions of piety in the *fiestas* – who was I to pass judgement on them, like a Pharisee?

Again, 'by chance' I went to Fatima and Lourdes in different professional connections in May 2001. In Fatima my children were again the sceptics: What proof is there of the apparitions, they inquired. 'How do you know it is true', they said to our Portugese hosts. 'We certainly do not believe in such things. Children make up all sorts of things, that we know for sure.'

The story of Fatima is fascinating, even to the toughest of pagans. Three small shepherd children from extremely modest backgrounds were tending to their sheep in the pasture. A lady from heaven appeared to them. She talked to them in their own dialect, and told them to come back on the thirteenth day of each month. The youngest child told her mother of the apparition. Soon the whole community knew. The clerical authorities, the press, and the whole of Europe was both scandalised and fascinated. The children were interrogated and their families suffered. Sceptics went in droves on the thirteenth day of the month to see for themselves. The children alone saw the lady, but on the last thirteenth day in 1917, all the 70,000 gathered there experienced the sun falling and moving abnormally, and were struck with fear.

The lady had told the two youngest children, Jacinta

and Francisco, that they would die very soon. This happened within a year's time. The oldest, Lucia, was told that she would live for a long time to tell about the secrets of Fatima revealed to her by the lady in white. She was finally to die on 13 February 2005 at the age of ninety-seven.

In May 2000 the Pope chose to reveal the contents of the third secret of Fatima. It had always been known to him and other popes. It *inter alia* predicted that a 'bishop in white' would be shot at. An assassination attempt was made on the Pope's life on 13 May 1981, the date of the Fatima apparations, and he said that the bullet which was shot at his heart was pushed aside by Our Lady of Fatima. The fact is that this very bullet changed course, inexplicably. This was bullet-proof, if you will.

That bullet is now in the crown of the statue of Our Lady of Fatima. The Pope was certain that she saved his life.

Our children are impressed. They look at the graves of the small children inside the basilica and notice that they were only ten and eleven years old when they died. They also see that the grave for Lucia is already prepared next to her siblings.

'Do you really believe this?' they once more ask our hosts. The man says: 'My mother was here at the last apparition herself, being thirteen years old then. It was 13 October 1917. She saw the sun rotate and almost fall down; they all thought it was the end of the world. What she and others saw, is at least certain: that the sun could not make these movements by itself.'

As we drive back to Lisbon, my twelve-year-old son Francis suddenly says: 'Look at the sky, mother! There is a light coming down from heaven, just like in Fatima!' We investigate through the car window, only to ascertain that this is to be explained by meterological science.

But I think to myself that the ones with prejudice are the ones who shut out the very possibility that the apparitions of Fatima really happened. To the eye of the unbeliever, there is no explanation that is fully satisfactory. But to the eye of the believer, it is not crucial to believe in this. Why should it be strange that God reveals himself in such ways to the small, simple children who have a pure heart? I am reminded of the Gospel text which simply says: 'He did not perform many miracles there as they had so little faith.'

And the 'empirical' fact is that thousands and thousands come to pray for the intercession of Mary at Fatima. Their faith is real enough.

It is mine that is more shaky.

The everyday miracle in Lourdes

As it happened, I came to Lourdes with the Scandinavian chapter of the Order of Malta; this time on pilgrimage. Again I felt out of place, and had my prejudices about such a place. At home someone said: 'Don't tell me you believe in those superstitions!' I said: 'One thing is certain: I am not superstitious, but I may still have prejudices. So I will go and see for myself with an open mind. But I dislike the Catholic Kitsch of the many shops as much as anyone.'

True, here you can find the most tasteless of all madonnas, in all shapes and colours: plastic figurines with blinking lights as halos around the head, and rosaries amidst all sorts of cheap junk jewellery. It is all very ugly, and all very human. Where there is a market, there will be goods for sale. But one must rise above this and ignore it.

Lourdes is situated at the foot of the Pyrenees, in breathtaking natural scenery. The mountain peaks are higher than in Norway, and more attractive. I had walked in the mountains on the Spanish side, and now looked longingly for the heights. But this time there was no occasion to take off.

Like in Fatima, Our Lady revealed herself to a poor child. Bernadette came from a very poor family which lived in what had been a prison cell in town, her father having gone bankrupt. It is a moving story to hear how the fourteen-year-old girl, too poor to go to school, went out to look for wood for the stove. This she had to do every day. She passed by the river which also runs through the town today. By the river bank there is a little grotto where she went in. Here a lady in white appeared to her, smiling and speaking her own dialect. The lady appeared several times, and Bernadette told her family and the local clergy about these apparitions. They disbelieved her, she was persecuted and interrogated, and hordes of people came to see the apparitions. It was only Bernadette who saw the lady, but the others saw clearly how her face was changing. She did strange and frightening things, like smearing the mud of the grotto on her face, telling the onlookers that it would be a healing source. The lady finally revealed her identity, saying in the local dialect, 'I am the immaculate conception' – the dogma which had recently been proclaimed. Bernadette did not know any of this herself, being completely unschooled; and the clerics were astonished. Shortly thereafter a spring of water appeared in the grotto, and the water is said to heal the sick. A thorough investigation finally concluded, in 1862, that the apparitions were authentic. Bernadette became a nun and died young, at thirty-six. She was canonised in 1933.

In the years afterwards, Lourdes became the place of pilgrimage for the sick. Some of these are healed in miraculous ways. A commission investigates such claims with two independent medical examinations: an international commission and a French commission of doctors. It is extremely difficult to have a miracle confirmed, given the natural scepticism in these cases. Several miracles of healing have been confirmed, following a long investigation. Many are still pending: An Irish Knight of Malta tells me that he experienced that someone in his group who was lame, could walk after his visit to Lourdes, but this case is still under investigation several years afterwards.

Believe or not believe in this? It is not really of key importance. I find it most likely, given the evidence, so to speak, that the apparitions here are true.

But there is another kind of 'evidence' here that is more important: The 'joie de vivre'.

The joy of life in this place is remarkable. We all push

wheelchairs. We all joke. The disfigured and the sick are in our midst, are part of our community. One is a young teenage girl with Downs syndrome. Another is an old retarded Italian lady who holds my hand all evening. A third has a damaged face and will never look 'normal' again. Many, many are old and in wheelchairs. There is an armada here of sick and old people. How can we be so happy together?

In 'normal' western settings one would even be disgusted at the sight of these people, shying away from them.

We all proceed to the church in a long row of wheel chairs. The natural beauty of the place is stunning: the mountains, the streamy river, the vale with with echoing churchbells. All this is an occasion for joy, but it is not the explanation for our joy here.

What makes us happy, is this: here we are all united as human beings in front of our common father, God. We are here to pray and sing His praise, asking for pardon and 'healing' through the intercession of Mary. We are just His children; sick or 'normal', lame or walking. He loves us all, and created us just as we are now. He sees that His creatures are beautiful, that we all bear His imprint, are His own willed children. We feel ourselves loved in a way that no human love can match. This reality makes us wildly happy.

But there is more: because we realise that we all bear His image, we do not see each other as 'normal' or sick, as more or less 'perfect'. This is an insight that sets us completely *free*: we are able to accept and love each other as we are. The dignity of the little girl with Downs is suddenly quite obvious. She shares as much in human dignity as I do. The old man in the wheel chair is perhaps much more human than I am in terms of imitating Christ.

The outer, physicial features become unimportant in Lourdes. The inner man becomes important, is transcending the body. The attachment to the bodily appearance is prominent in secular society: we all judge each other by appeareance: are you young, slim, attractive? Or are you

useless, old, and sick? The disappearance of the handicapped through abortion makes this trend even more
pronounced: they simply disappear before they are born.
Increasingly we do not interact any more with fellow
human beings who are sick. We look upon them as abnormal, as 'sub-optimal', as having *less dignity* than us.

Here is it the opposite. There are as many sick as others,
perhaps more. And the sickness is unimportant in the
sense that we do not notice it. It is not what counts in our
relationship with God. This is the only right perspective
on life and the other. It is striking to me how the word
human dignity takes on its right meaning here in Lourdes.
Dignity is not about appearance; it is about personhood. It
makes no sense unless you see God as the author of the
human person, but then, when you realise this, you see
Him in especially the sick and the old.

Then love between human beings enters. Your hard
heart is pierced by a love for this other who is weak and
sick, and you are ashamed about your own self-centredness.

Love is not what you thought it was, connected to
appearance and attractiveness. Love is God Himself. You
catch a glimpse of this love in your sudden and surprising
joy in Lourdes, from singing and praying with some
invalids whom you push around in a wheelchair.

That is the real miracle you will experience here, worth
more than any apparition to the hardened hearts of
modern man.

We are in the process of eliminating the sick and old, the
handicapped and the weak – unborn as well as born. This
dehumanisation of the western world stands in complete
and stark contrast to the concept of human dignity.
Dignity is the 'finger-print' of the Lord on us. When we elim-
inate those who are unlike us, we kill the Lord as well. The
everyday miracle in Lourdes is the joy of being the
beloved, imperfect children He has made us, knowing that
He loves us in all shapes and forms. There is a tremendous
freedom in this; a joy that is completely hidden from
modern western man.

Did I come closer to Mary in Lourdes? Perhaps. We shall see. The torchlight procession in the evening was a solemn, moving ceremony. I was struck by the seriousness and dignity of the participants: wheel chairs, helpers, lay people, clergy – reciting the rosary and the sorrowful mysteries. I thought about little Bernadette who was so simple and unschooled; how she was persecuted on account of her visions. Is it at all likely that she made it up? What about the later healings of the infirm? The final recognition of the Church, which is always very sceptical about such occurrences? If you consider the evidence in our empirical sense, it is solid. By sheer human logic one would most likely conclude, here as in Fatima, that the apparitions are true.

But ultimately it is not this logic that is important. It is rather to have an open mind and a humble heart. Lourdes, Fatima, Santiago are places you should go to renew your inner life, through atonement for your sins in order to make a new beginning. In Lourdes all the sick help you to achieve this, for they make you see your own hardness of heart so well.

Mary the mother speaks to me as a mother: how we should love the weak and small; how motherly love is tender and merciful. To care for the sick is intimately connected with motherhood, and in Lourdes this specific dignity shines forth. The strength of the feminine is so clear: Mary can never be associated with weakness. Meekness is its very opposite.

The sorrowful myseries tell a tale of extreme strength in a mother whose son was mutilated and killed before her very eyes, but it is the strength of being the 'hand-maiden of the Lord' without conditions which reveals the utmost perfection and strength a human being can have. She loved Christ the way we should love Him, and this love was self-giving, not demanding anything. But she is also the model of motherly love among humans: I could cry when I think about how she loved her Son, like I love my sons; and how she had to stand aside when He suffered more than any human being. Which mother can bear this? So many mothers have suffered like this, losing their children, having no way to help, but being able to love until the end.

In all Finnish Lutheran churches there is a framed letter from General Mannerheim, in command of the Finnish army during the Winter War in 1943. It it to the Finnish mothers, thanking them for their sacrifice for Finland. They lost their sons in that terrible war. Usually no one thinks about the silent mothers and their suffering for love.

For me Mary is to be imitated as woman and as human being, that much I know now. *She knew how to love, like no other human being.* This can be deduced on a purely human logic. The rest – her role in the spiritual life of so many – I have yet to penetrate more fully. But I have rid myself of some more prejudices in Lourdes. The many millions who come here every year in devotion to Mary, asking for her intercession, do not have my prejudices. They have probably known her all their lives.

As my friend said, 'Tell her that you don't know her.' Perhaps it is that simple after all. I will try.

Human Love is a way to God

To love Christ is the condition for being a Christian, for being able to be transformed into a Christian person. To discover what love is starts with human love, like the motherly love for children is the way to understanding Mary's love for her son, and in turn His love for us.

In Norway, everyone is familar with *Kristin Lavransdatter*, the trilogy that won Undset the Nobel prize for literature in 1928. Kristin is the woman we recognise. She lived in medieval Norway, but was nonetheless one of us. She was headstrong, passionate, impatient, and matured slowly through suffering and hardship. She fought with God until the end of her life – her will against His will. She lived in nature, close to nature; lived life in full. She loved the man who turns out to disappoint her.

All women long for a man like Erlend, despite his faults. Undset describes his stature, his good looks, his muscles, his bravery. We fall in love with Erlend. He is manhood, at least physical manhood.

Kristin is womanhood. Her life as woman and mother is depicted in the most realistic way. When I was pregnant with my first child, I suddenly recalled the way Kristin understood that she was pregnant: one day in the wood, she suddenly felt a movement like that of a fish in water, a faint stirring inside her. It is exactly like that. I remember sitting in the living room, about twenty weeks pregnant, but only knowing it theoretically. Then, all of a sudden, such a movement in my womb! The first sign of my child. I'll never forget that moment.

When Undset describes Kristin's labour and childbirth, it is also true to life. The first birth almost kills her. The pain for hours, the fear of dying, the utter horror of the situation. Some woman attending her; and Erlend, weak and cowardly. After a day and a night, when she thinks she is dying, the child is finally born. He is described as a lump of bloody flesh. He is her first-born son.

I think women recognise themselves in this description of a normal, real childbirth. It is horrible, it is not romantic. It is painful unto death, and it requires the utmost of your physical and psychological strength.You risk your life for another life. You partake in creation. Therefore it is the most profound experience of your life.

Kristin's author was a realist in every sense of the word. What she writes about human love, about childbirth, about our struggle with God, about the human condition, is real. Here we find no ornamentations, prudishness or theoretical considerations. Here we find life itself.

Undset, who is my most important inspiration, refused to play any roles. Life is too serious and short for that. I never knew her personally – she died in 1949, before I was born, but she left traces everywhere.

In one of the earliest novels, *Jenny*, from 1911, she describes a journey to Rome. Jenny lives there with friends from Norway, all painters. She falls in love, gets married, has children. But the husband turns out to disappoint her. He is not the man she looked for and dreamed of. This theme recurs in Undset's writings, and I believe it to be autobiographical. She longed for a real man in the sense of a courageous and virtuous man – a noble man. Such men she found in the sagas, in European literature, but not in her own life. Like Jenny, she married a painter, Hans Svarstad, and had three children by him. One of them was retarded. The marriage was a failure and they parted in 1919 – the year the third child was born.

This search for true and noble love is also the *Leitmotiv* for *Kristin Lavransdatter*. It is not surprising that it finally led to Christianity. The search for true love has to be, finally, a supernatural search, although one may find human beings that are capable of such love. They are the men who have acquired the human virtues, and perhaps also the supernatural ones. Kristin's father Lavrans is such a man: strong and just; an attractive man because he has the depth and seriousness of a full life of faith. Erlend is attractive physically, humanly, but is lacking depth and maturity.

Here I want to recall her realism again. She never made the error of separating mind and body. The love Kristin offered and sought, was a total love, physical as well as of the mind. She loved Erlend the person: physical love was an integral part of love itself, of her self-giving to him. Kristin is pregnant before she gets married, but this was almost a natural consequence of loving Erlend fully. She gave herself to him, but he was unable to appreciate it. This was her human tragedy, one that gradually led her to seek and find total love in Christ. But this quest was in no way a harmonious or easy one. She was tormented by her own strong will, by her natural and very human demand that she should find this love in a man, that this love be of this world – tangible, and physical.

The realism of human love is that its fullness is a love of both body and soul, of the two together. Prudishness is totally foreign to Undset. She knows human nature. The strength of natural human passion is such that we fight against ourselves for much of our lives, unless we have found the other who fulfils us. Few indeed are those who find such another.

But gradually we may come to discover two things: that human suffering can be borne and can be a means to sanctity; and also that there is a path, well hidden, to perfect love. This path is Christ, and the mystery of divine love. Kristin ends her quest on a pilgrimage to Nidaros to atone for her sins. Her rebelliousness and strong will finally accept God's primacy, and she abandons herself to Him. But it is the end of a long journey of resistence, so much like our own.

This is how human life is. It is full of passion, of sorrow, of failures. Kristin can only abandon herself when she has put up every struggle against God.

Conversion

Undset wrote two books, a sequel, about converting in Norway; largely, we may presume, autobiograhical. *Gymnadenia* appeared in 1929; its sequel, *Den brennende busk* ('The Burning Bush'), in 1930. Paul Selmer, the main character, is unhappily married, leads a petit-bourgeois existence, and is drawn to the Catholic Church through studies and literature. He converts against the will of his family and friends. He is married to the boring and very conventional Bjørg, who is both childish and snobbish. The marriage is a failure. Then he meets his one-time love, Lucy, and realises that she is the woman of this life. He loves Lucy, and this fact will remain. He is married to a stupid, superficial woman and also this fact remains. He is despairing over his fate, and collapses before the Tabernacle in all his human misery. From the human perspective, there is in fact no way out. He has no hope unless he believes. At this point Undset relates how Paul is helped by God, in a spiritual experience there in St Olav's church in Oslo. He has a vision of a burning bush, and he understands that this is God's grace and help to him. He accepts and tries to love his fate.

This book by Undset has the same theme as Kristin's: the depth of human sorrow and passion, and the simultaneous search for love that is fulfilling more than what human love can offer. True, in a human person one may find a total love – in the rare case of finding another self, a *Seelenfreund*. But the quest for love goes further; it points at the existence of God. But man is so stubborn that he or she has to exhaust all human power and willpower before one is ready for the surrender to God. Paul Selmer thinks that God will fit into his plans and his little bourgeois universe. But no, God tries him and seemingly leaves him in a state of human hopelessness before he restores him. Only when Paul realises that the woman he loves is unattainable and that he must stay married to the awful Bjørg is he ready to make the real choice for Christ. He cannot rely on himself anymore because he is desperately unhappy and there is no way out for him.

The dramatic struggle against oneself and one's natural and very human passions is realism. Undset never underestimated human nature, its rebelliousness and its strength. A life lived to the full is a life where none of this in unknown, but where one makes a choice and dares to fight a battle.

Undset's relevance

The realism I speak about here is not only realism in a philosophical and theological sense. It is also the realism of seeing human nature as it is. Today we cannot even speak about human nature as a given. We live in a time which is extremely nihilistic, where atomistic individuals often relate to no one but themselves. Undset discovered that God exists outside herself, and the implication of this for her was to submit to Him. Until this discovery she certainly had explored human nature profoundly. One can hardly discover God without knowing human nature. We find God through self-knowledge. He is not an abstract idea, but our Father.

Today we seem to have lost knowledge of both God and

human nature. The human being is self-sufficient and even completely autonomous from other people. We have no need of God, and the only aspect of life we still do not control, is death. That is, we can control its onset through euthansia and suicide, but not that it will occur. This fact bothers us so much that we suppress it as best we can.

Undset is so relevant because she describes life as it really is. Her characters are men and woman who live naturally. They are born, they work, they love, they struggle, they die. They seek meaning in life. They may find God. They are thoroughly normal people. The spiritual quest is part of a normal human life.

Recently I went to the funeral of my great-uncle. He was a farmer and fisherman in southern Norway, living in the tradition of lay Christianity I described above. It was a moving event because it is was so real. He worked hard to feed his big family, and he spent his free time as an organist in the *bedehus* of the village. His grandchildren and great-grandchildren put flowers on his coffin. His son bade him farewell, and we all 'followed' him to the grave. The word 'follow' is used in Norwegian when someone is buried. One accompanies the deceased on his last journey. The priest spoke about the transition from this life: 'Your days are numbered. Learn to count your days.' We sang about generations following generations.

The realism contained in this funeral is true to human nature. We live for a short while, we have a task on this earth, then we die and are chaff. A human life is short, and the body dies all the time – a little day by day. How can we live as if death will not come; as if we would live forever here when we know this? The way most people live today is thoroughly unrealistic.

It is as if Undset wanted to imprint on us: life is not what you think it is. You are but one link in a long chain of generations, and your most real experience is to give birth, to father children, to love another person, and most of all, to love God. Reality is to be tempted, to fight, to fail, to get up again. Natural life leads to supernatural life – human life lived fully leads to the search for God. For instance, her descriptions of motherhood and its importance are extremely powerful. Motherhood and family are natural institutions, and the experience of being a mother makes it possible for us to know the Holy Family. The natural is the way to the supernatural.

Love and Sex

Love is sex, and sex is love. This seems a common assumption today. But love and sex often have nothing to do with each other at all: the urge for an orgasm is a biological drive we all have, and sex can and is carried out without any reference to love most of the time. Then it is just that: satisfaction of this biological need; good while it lasts, but nothing more.

Sex as an expression of love is something much more; something sublime. It is a self-giving, a deep way to say that 'I love you with my whole being'. This self-giving is also a unity of two bodies, becoming as it were, and as it written in Scripture, 'one flesh'. Because this deep unity of a mutual self-giving represents a total commitment of one person to another, the Church treats sex with such respect and seriousness. When sex expresses love as self-giving, as union, it is much more than sex as self-satisfaction. Marriage is therefore the proper context, especially because the mystery of new life emerges from this sexual unity.

Today's hypocrisy about love and sex is nauseating. Why pretend that sex has anything to do with love when it demonstrably has not in most cases? Why think that sex will bring you love when it usually won't? Sex as satisfaction is plain and simple enough; it is a drive and a need, but one which can be controlled. Many don't think that it can, and will not even try; and that goes for both men and women. But sex is basically a very *simple* matter, completely overrated in importance today, and made into perversions in order to give a 'kick' in societies where ordinary sex has become deflated and boring.

But love is an entirely different thing, and sex is only

relevant to love when love is there in the first place. One does not love because one has sex, but may only have sex because one loves. But love is much more than the physical expression between man and woman: it is what makes the human being happy in this life.

Kristin looked for the noble in a man to love, and was disappointed; she was on the right path nonetheless. We naturally love the noble, the virtuous – as I loved what was noble in the books I read as a young girl. The physical attraction of a man, his masculinity – yes, by all means; a tremendous force, but even more so, his qualities: his virtues, which is what is noble in him.

This nobility points to Christ, for it is an imitation of His perfection. Human virtue is the way to imitate Him. Herein lies the secret of human and divine love; their meeting-point. In order to fall in love, we must become attracted. We are, unless we are really corrupted, attracted by nobility in another person.

Love is however not about being in love, seeing the beloved. It is the necessary start. Love is about persevering and giving of oneself. There is a big difference: the being in love is possessive, wanting to be with the beloved; not caring about others. But loving implies opening up to suffering and service. Like a marriage that starts with being in love, and if it lasts, it is marked by persevering, accepting the faults of the other, and despite this, loving him and others in the family. Such love is less and less self-centred, and more and more self-giving. The model for this true love is Christ and his outpouring of love for us, all of those indifferent people, unto death, conditionless.

In human terms this is not possible. We need the constant 'support' from God for our own feeble love; the love He pours out on us becomes the source of strength for us, and enables us to imitate Him in loving others – all those whom we otherwise, by human effort, never would have been able to love. 'The love of Christ forces us', as the Salvation Army sister said.

Undset's view of sexuality was also decidedly 'unmodern'. Sexuality is a wonderful, deep expression of self-giving, is fundamental to love between man and woman, and is something mysterious and secluded. The fact that a child is conceived by this activity makes it in a sense divine. She would have hated the trivialisation of sex in our time which kills the erotic element completely. In Scandinavia the trend towards 'demystification' of sex has been very pronounced, and began in her time by the insistence on sexual education in schools. She remarked, in her essays entitled *Et Kvinnesynspunkt* ('A Woman's Point of View', 1922), that the 'prophets' of sexuality as biology robbed sexuality of its meaning and beauty.

In our time there is no debate more needed than a debate about sexual ethics. To many people this would appear a contradiction in terms. Indeed, one of the prophets of 'free' sex in Norway was once given a distinction which came with a motto. The motto was *cogito, ergo sum*, which was immediately remade by some wit to be *coitus, ergo sum*.

The sexual boredom of today has a lot to do with the growth of sexual perversion, as the plain, old heterosexual act between steady partners seems outdated. We live in an 'over-sexed' time where there is no other meaning of sex than mechanical pleasure, for which one does not even need a partner. How far we are from the beautiful love and erotic attraction that Kristin felt for Erlend! How far we are from the obvious connection between sex and conception, sex and the mysterious possibility of creation! The wonder of the sexual union is lost when sex no longer expresses anything or carries with it the sublime and almost divine aspect of partaking in the making of new life.

Undset did not live to hear of the abortion debate. I am glad of that. I can imagine her scorn and anger. For her, natural and supernatural human life was centred on the transmission of life by strong men and women, and she resisted any politicisation of the family and especially of motherhood. Looking at her large number of books, it strikes me that the two most central themes are human love reaching and struggling towards divine love, and motherhood. When I wrote my own reflections on feminism[1] I was inspired by her clear and consistent anthropology in this respect. One can almost see how she moved from a preoccupation with human nature and its passions to the supernatural plane which offers the only 'resolution' of human longing and suffering.

But today we do not get the anthropology right at all. We think that masculinity and feminity are constructed, imagined 'roles' that can be learned and unlearned, likewise that sexuality is a construct of society and malleable, and that sexuality has no relation to creation. We debase sexuality and thereby pervert it. It no longer has any place in any relationship. Likewise, we think that the family is a nominal, not an essential institution. Here we are back to the damage done by nominalism: there is no essence of things, only their 'nomos', which means name. There is no ontological realism, only the names we give things. The things in themselves do not necessarily exist. There is no objective institution called the family, only what we call a family.

If there is no God who exists independently of us, then we must discard God altogether. In such a universe – which is the *Zeitgeist* of Scandinavia and much of the western world now – logically there can be no objective reality for anything else. If the *Grundbegriffe* are totally relativistic, all is subjective. Therefore Undset's religious realism is tied to her realism about human nature. The two hang together. First she made a total inventory of human nature, and then – logically – ended in the Catholic Church once she posed the essential question: 'Is there a God outside my subjective opinion of this matter?'

Conversely, today when God is no longer needed by most people, the same people do not know what human nature is. Human nature, in its fallen state, is also God-like. Human life is a struggle between good and evil, to the last day. But today we think that the human being is self-sufficient, master of himself and of the universe. All that

[1] *A Time to Blossom*, Mondadori, 1999.

we can imagine doing, we do; and we not only do it, but claim to have a right to do it. We are probably farther from knowing ourselves than any generations before us. To Christians, life is a gradual improvement in knowing oneself. To those who think we are perfect, this idea is absurd.

Real Love

Undset gives us a chance to start all over again. She does not speak about God, secularisation, theology, or philosophy. Instead, she describes our human nature. We identify with Kristin. We fall in love with Erlend. We admire Lavrans. Why? Because they are real human beings, with passions, sins, failures, greatness, courage. They show us what human virtue and human vice is. We follow Kristin as young girl and mother, we remember the drama of our own birth when see her labour, and we gradually understand that the human being seeks happiness and love outside herself, to be found in the hidden God when we follow her painful pilgrimage to Nidaros.

Today there are few lucky enough to grow up in strong families where they are taught what a virtuous life is. My relative who was buried recently, was the head of such a family. His sons knew that they worked and prayed, that they helped those who have less; that God would come when they least expected it. Theirs has been a life of consistency and unity – none of them especially gifted or bright, but all of them ethically sound. Life is to work, to form a family, to live by the word of God. When you die, you should be prepared. Your Lord is expecting you. You come from dust and return to dust.

This realism is as far from the modern western person as it can be. With our self-centredness, we need to hear personal testimony, best of all to experience it all ourselves. We can imagine this question posed to Undset: 'What does it mean to live a meaningful life?' She would probably point to her books: read and find out.

My relatives, not rich, not especially talented, not famous, not educated: they lead a meaningful life although they have never reflected on it. Neither have they reflected on whether God exists, whether the family exists, whether sexuality is socially constructed, or whether they should work for the family and help their neighbours. They have simply lived a natural life imbued with the fear of God.

God and man hang together. When we forget who God is, we also forget who man is.

A way back to the discovery of human nature is Undset because her characters captivate. All her polemical articles, part of the societal debate, are good, but her novels are far better. People do not learn from logic, but look for someone with whom to identify. If they find Kristin and Erlend, they are on the way. Undset the intellectual appeals to me, but Undset the storyteller is much greater. She is a woman for all seasons.

In the Norwegian national anthem it says: '*Også kvinner op at stride, som de vore menn*' – 'Also women took up arms in battle, as if they were men.' This is not strength; it is easy. Strength is to know yourself as a woman, as a man, as a person, and to recognise that you are a child of God. In short, to dare to live a full life.

Love with deeds

A Saturday in June. It is the best time of the year in Norway. After a long, hard winter with darkness all day and cold, frozen earth, nature is alive again. The birds celebrate with singing. It is green, sunny, fresh. I would never trade the dramatic change of seasons for a better climate farther south. Up here you learn the importance of the weather and the hardship of nature.

It is as if creation is born anew each spring. In March the snow starts to melt; it is still cold and gloomy, and you can still ski in Oslo. In April the snow must give in, and there are some days of sun and a few green spots, perhaps even warm days. But it is treacherous – it can snow, it can be very cold. But then, in May and June, winter is dead until October. There is no turning back to it. It is green, and we dare to plant the flowers for summer. Until late May we wait, counting the days. 'Is the night frost gone?' we ask each other. If you make a mistake there, all your expensive flowers are dead if there is yet another night with 'frost', which means below zero degrees.

One can only appreciate nature's reawakening when there is death, winter. The tombstones fall over once the melting starts and *'telen går av jorda'* – when the frost leaves the ground after many months of winter. The frozen earth is dead, and spring comes each year like a miracle. The parable of the mustard seed has its Norwegian equivalent: the lifeless earth cannot give life by itself. It is dead – there is no life in it. But then it starts to give life nonetheless. The human eye does not see why, yet it happens each year.

The human being can be alive, too, in abundance, but this life does not come from the human being itself. The human being can only be ready and open to this life; in a word, be humble, but this in turn is the very precondition for real life. This key human virtue is the condition for Christ's life in us. Not surprisingly, the Latin word for humble is *humilis*, derived from *humus*, meaning earth.

This Saturday in June I was outside Oslo, in the country-side. The hills were green, the sky blue, with swift winds moving the clouds. The freshness of this pastoral landscape is very different from the permanent warmth and sun-dried countryside of southern Europe. It is a sudden freshness, a new life, nature awake after the frozen stillness. This change of seasons is abrupt, and almost shocking to us. We are so happy each year; the smells are new, the sun is back. Finally, finally, after all those months inside!

We relish this closeness with nature. The farm animals that are let out after winter inside the barn behave like they are crazy; half-blindly jumping around in the meadows. Sometimes I compare ourselves to them: we go out in the fields and woods, praising nature and smelling the newborn dark earth. Norwegians, most of them half-pagan, have one insight about God: He is in nature. 'I find God in nature' , they always say. There is some truth in that.

But this day was not one for an outing. It was rather the opposite of new life from the earth: it was dead life becoming earth. It was the funeral of a friend.

He died after an operation, from complications. He was himself a surgeon, and a very good one at that. And he was a man of quiet virtue. He had come to Norway in 1956, like my husband, as a refugee from Communist Hungary. He had fought in Budapest during those fateful October days, and had killed his guards in order to escape.This necessity of survival was not easy to live with later, especially as he killed in a way that left the guards no chance. He had hidden a piano string, tied around his leg. The guards missed it in the search. That was fatal for them.

In Norway, he married a local girl and had four children. They were grown by now. In the funeral ceremony his sons were going to talk, and persisted, despite the crying which they could not stop. The widow said but a sentence: 'You have given me so much love during these forty years together.'

There were others who talked about his service: medical colleagues and fellow Hungarians. What they in fact talked about were deeds done out of love.

This summer day, when life was reborn from the earth; he was gone. Death was sudden, as it often is. We seldom understand why it happens when it happens. It seems that the good ones die. They leave so much sorrow. We will never understand why they had to die just then. But this man had left traces of his life – he had loved with deeds. He was a Catholic, but not very practising. Yet his ethos remained that of human virtue: to perform one's professional duty well, to serve one's family and country. He did so in a quiet manner; his colleagues and patients testifying to his friendship and respect in addition to his ability in surgery; and his countrymen and distinctions testifying to his courage for his country. Then the most eloquent testimony of all: his family's deep sorrow and dignified farewell. It moved every heart, and it also told us that he had loved them with his deeds all his grown life.

No more time for doing good deeds, for learning how to love. His time was up.

What was the point of it all? What was the one thing necessary? The one thing necessary is to love in this life; to love in the right way: not possessive, craving, self-centred love, but outpouring, self-giving love in imitation of Christ. It may take a whole lifetime to learn how to love in the right way, but each effort is a step on this way. The redemption of the world, the reincarnation of the world and all its people, is somehow, mysteriously, dependent on us, on God's own creatures. He wants our cooperation and effort. We will not see the result of this and we cannot measure the progress towards this goal, for we live short lives and have limited vision. We are blinded by original sin and our own sins; they are like an illness of the eyes, as Undset said. But we can nevertheless learn how to love in the company and imitation of Christ, helped by the sacraments. To strive to love like He did, that is the meaning and purpose of this life. He will take care of the rest. But loving Him and loving others is the key, the one thing necessary.

When this short life is up, we, too, must have left some traces. Other people may not see them at all, but that is not important. God is the hidden God, and love is the hidden force that makes human life really human.

Hidden, but powerful; like the transformation of frozen earth into blossoming gardens each spring.

www.ingramcontent.com/pod-product-compliance
Lightning Source LLC
Chambersburg PA
CBHW022017090426
42739CB00006BA/181